PRESIDENTIAL ADDRESSES ON ARAB-ISLAMIC STUDIES

PRESIDENTIAL ADDRESSES ON ARAB-ISLAMIC STUDIES

Prof. Dr. Abdul Ali
Department of Islamic Studies
AMU, Aligarh

KITAB BHAVAN
NEW DELHI-110002

Kitab Bhavan
Publishers, Distributors, Exporters & Importers
1784, Kalan Mahal, Darya Ganj
New Delhi-110002 (India)

Phone : (91-11) 3277392/93, 3274686
Web Site : www.kitabbhavan.com
E-mail : nasri@vsnl.com
Fax : (91-11) 3263383

First Edition ... 2002

ISBN : 81-7151-340-2
Book Code : P00158

Laser Typesetting at:
Laser Track
Darya Ganj, New Delhi-2

Published in India by:
Nusrat Ali Nasri for Kitab Bhavan
1784, Kalan Mahal, Darya Ganj
New Delhi-110002 [India]

Printed in India at:
Nice Printing Press
Khureji Khas, Delhi-110051

CONTENTS

Preface VII

Foreword IX

1. Presidential Address: West Asian Studies Section 29th Session, A.I.O.C., Poona (1978) 1

2. Presidential Address: Arabic and Persian Section 31st Session, A.I.O.C., Jaipur (1982) 15

3. Presidential Address: Islamic Studies Section 32nd Session, A.I.O.C., Ahmedabad (1985) 27

4. Presidential Address: Islamic Studies Section 33rd Session, A.I.O.C., Calcutta (1986) 45

5. Presidential Address: Islamic Studies Section 35th Session, A.I.O.C., Hardwar (1990) 61

6 Presidential Address: Arabic and Persian Section 37th Session, A.I.O.C., Rohtak (1994) 81

7. Presidential Address: Islamic Studies Section 38th Session, A.I.O.C., Jadavpur (1997) 99

8. Presidential Address: Islamic Studies Section 39th Session, A.I.O.C., Vadodara (1998) 117

9. Presidential Address: South-East Asian Studies Section, 40th Session, A.I.O.C., Chennai (2000) 131

Index 141

Dedicated to those who do the deeds of justice and righteousness

PREFACE

The All-India Oriental Conference, a premier Body of Orientalists in India, was brought into existence in 1919 through the initiative and efforts of the Bhandarkar Oriental Research Institute, Poona. It was founded with the main aim of coordinating the academic pursuits of scholars working in the diverse branches of Oriental Studies. The first session of the Conference held at Poona on 5-7 November, 1919, was inaugurated by the then governor of Bombay George Lloyads and presided over by Sir R.G. Bhandarkar, the renowned Indian Orientalist and social reformer. It has since been bringing together at one platform scholars of Oriental Studies from all over the country every alternate year.

Arabic and Persian Section was included in the programme of the Conference since its very inception, the first Sectional President of which was Prof. S. Khuda Bukhsh, an eminent scholar of Arabic and Islamic Studies. Sanskrit language and literature, Avesta, Pali, Buddhism, Ancient History, Philosophy, etc., were other important subjects of discussion at the first session of the Conference. In the course of time several other disciplines were added to it including the Sections of Islamic Studies, West Asian Studies, and South-East Asian Studies.

I have been closely associated with the All-India Oriental Conference since 1968 when its 24th Session was held under the auspices of the Varanaseya Sanskrit University at Varanasi. I also have had the honour of presiding over different sections of the Conference several times. And the present volume is a collection of the Presidential Addresses presented by me on these occasions. Since these Addresses are in-depth studies on hitherto neglected but important topics of Arab-Islamic learning, it is hoped that the book will be useful for both students and scholars of Oriental Studies in general and of Islamic Studies and allied subjects in particular.

Lastly, I wish to express my hearty thanks to my friend and inspirer Prof. N. Akmal Ayyubi, former Chairman, Deptt. of Islamic Studies, A.M.U., Aligarh, for having yielded to my persistent requests to write his scholarly foreword to this volume. My thanks are also due to Prof. M.S. Agwani, former Vice-Chancellor, Jawahar Lal Nehru University, New Delhi, for having gone through the West Asian Studies Presidential Address and given his encouraging remarks before its presentation. I am also thankful to Mr. Syed Ausaf Ali, former director of the Indian Institute of Islamic Studies (now Hamdard University), New Delhi, for having given me his valuable ideas as well as provided me with the facilities of studies and research at his Institute where the fourth Presidential Address was prepared. Finally, I should like to thank Mr. Kabir Ahmad Khan, Assistant Librarian at the Institute of Islamic Studies, Aligarh Muslim University, Aligarh, whose vast bibliographical knowledge and efficient handling of books have been of great help to me.

Abdul Ali

FOREWORD

The All-India Oriental Conference which was originally called Indian Oriental Conference, has been serving for the last eighty years as the national forum of scholars interested in scientific Orientology. It was brought into existence for the purpose of co-ordinating and promoting the scholarly activities of individuals and institutions working in the field of Oriental Studies. Its sessions are normally held once every two years at different centres in the country and research papers are submitted, presented and discussed by scholars.

The All-India Oriental Conference has now firmly established itself as the authorised national forum of the Orientalists of India. At present the Conference is divided into sixteen sections including those of Islamic Studies, Arabic & Persian, West Asian Studies, and South-East Asian Studies. All these sections are presided over by eminent scholars and their Presidential Addresses are rich contributions to knowledge.

Prof. Abdul Ali has also presided over Islamic Studies, Arabic & Persian, West Asian Studies, and South-East Asian Studies Sections of the All-India Oriental Conference several times. A scholar of international repute, he has distinguished himself in his field of studies and research. The present volume is a collection of nine research articles on Arab-Islamic Studies which were presented as Presidential Addresses at different sections of the Conference. Since these Addresses are based on deep research and extensive investigations, it is hoped that this book will be hailed as a treasure for students and scholars of Arab-Islamic history and culture. Even the general educated readers will find it interesting and useful.

The first Presidential Address presented by Prof. Dr. Abdul Ali at the West Asian Studies Section of the 29th session of the

All-India Oriental Conference held at Poona in 1978, opens with an analytical account of the unique geo-strategic position of West Asia as the connecting link between the East and the West as well as gives a glimpse of the main historical factors that have shaped the destiny of this region through the ages. He also describes in detail why this area will always remain the centre-stage of international politics and power rivalry.

Touching on the age-old Indo-West Asian relations he highlights the fact that there has been a lively cultural and intellectual interchange between what the peoples of both regions possessed in different branches of knowledge and learning. He also focuses on geo-political reasons for further development of economic and political relations with the peoples of this area, thereby emphasizing the need for India to play a greater role in the vast market for technology, services, manpower and commercial goods that has opened up in all the oil-rich West Asian nations. Thus it is clearly indicated that there lies a vast potential for our country's participation in the industrial and technological development of these nations on mutually beneficial terms.

Finally, the address closes with specific suggestions and guidelines for the pursuit of studies and research in West Asian history, politics, sociology, and economics at some selected Indian universities where emphasis should be put on the need to study the modern thinkers and writers of West Asia in original rather than through the writings of Western scholars whose interpretations are but naturally coloured by their imperialistic motives.

His second Presidential Address presented at the Arabic and Persian Section of the 31st Session of the A.I.O. Conference held at the University of Rajasthan in 1982, contains a brief assessment of the part played by Arabic and Persian languages in the advancement of human knowledge and learning as well as of their contributions to the cultural heritage of India.

This address upholds the fact that the contributions made by Arab-Muslim scholars and scientists in different branches of knowledge such as philosophy, medicine, mathematics, physics, mineralogy, botany, geography, chemistry, fine arts, music, etc., form the connecting link between the Greco-Roman classical age and the modern civilization. It also discusses in detail some important aspects of Indo-Arab cultural and intellectual interchange through the ages.

Lastly, it focuses on the need to prepare general descriptive catalogues of various Arabic and Persian manuscripts that are lying scattered all over the world, as non-availability of such catalogues not only renders the works of research tedious and difficult, but also keeps the research scholars in the dark about the available source materials in their respective fields of studies.

The third Presidential Address was presented at the Islamic Studies Section of the 32nd Session of the A.I.O. Conference held under the auspices of the University of Gujarat at Ahmedabad in 1985. This is an important piece of original research work, in which an attempt has been made to give a critical reassessment of the mentality and legacy of the pre-Islamic Arabs with a view to presenting a realistic and balanced image of them rather than condemning them outright as a totally immoral, vicious and foolish lot. This enables the readers to understand in a better manner not only the type of stuff they constituted for the rise and growth of Islam, but also the subsequent development of its various institutions.

In conclusion, it has been clearly brought out on the basis of facts quoted from the Qur'ãn and pre-Islamic Arabic literature that the Arabs were an eloquent, brave and scientific people who had tremendous capacity for observation, assimilation and acclimatization. In short, the pre-Islamic Arabs have been presented as having been in possession of all the ingredients of a powerful nation which needed to be tamed, sharpened and channelized by a civilizing force. And that was the main reason that as soon as they became united under the banner of Islam, they emerged as a highly cultured and powerful nation, and contributed a great deal to human thought and progress in almost all fields of scientific and cultural activity.

The fourth Presidential Address was presented at the Islamic Studies Section of the 33rd Session of the A.I.O. Conference held under the auspices of the Asiatic Society, Calcutta, on October 24-26, 1986. It gives a detailed critical account of Western distortions of Islam and the motives behind it through the ages. This is followed by a discussion on the need to highlight the contributions of Islam to the advancement of science and civilization. Prof. Abdul Ali clearly points out that the mistrust about Islam in the West is not the result of independent thinking of the Western people, but rather it is motivated by their age-old hostile attitude towards this religion and its followers which was generated mainly by the triumph of Muslims over Jews and Christians in the Middle Ages. And that is the main reason why the vast body of literature on Islam produced by missionaries and their Orientalists is replete with grave and mischievous inaccuracies.

Barring a few examples, most of the Orientalists in the 18th and 19th centuries made Prophet Muhammad the main target of their attack, and painted him in the blackest of colours. Even the 20th century non-Muslim Orientalists fared no better than their predecessors. They tirelessly subjected the tenets of Islam to biased criticism by depicting it as the enemy of scientific thought and progress.

While rebutting the charges levelled by Western writers against Islam and Muslims, Dr. Abdul Ali maintains that Islam has been and remains a scientific way of living which aims at both spiritual uplift and material well-being of man. The tolerant and secular political spirit of Islam is described as another great contribution of this religious system to the growth of human civilization. The address also stresses the need to introduce the main ingredients of Islamic civilization in their proper perspectives to the modern scientific world which is confronted with a number of challenges that threaten the very stability of society. It further emphasizes that the scholars pursuing Islamic studies should undertake a systematic and comprehensive study of the contributions of Muslim scientists to the advancement of science with a view to properly assessing and evaluating their role as bearers of the torch of culture and civilization.

The address closes with a discussion on the traditions of Islamic learning being carried on in our traditional institutions and seminaries which not only teach and train students in the Islamic religious sciences, but also publish books and periodicals on them. Lamenting the wide gap that exists between the scholars of these traditional institutions and those of our modern universities, Prof. Abdul Ali rightly considers it desirable and imperative to bring about some sort of co-ordination and co-operation between both groups of scholars with a view to enabling them to carry on their works more efficiently.

The fifth Presidential Address was delivered at the Islamic Studies Section of the 35th Session of the A.I.O. Conference which was held at Hardwar under the auspices of the Gurukul Kangri Vishwavidyalaya, a great centre of Oriental Studies. It is devoted to the discussion of the hitherto little-studied but important aspects of the part played by Muslim scientists as harbingers of the modern scientific era.

At the outset, Dr. Abdul Ali gives an elaborate account of the scientific and intellectual foundations of Islam as repeatedly emphasized in the Qur'ãn which is described as the main source of inspiration for scientific investigation of Nature and natural phenomena. The main cause of the backwardness of the present-day Muslims in the domain of science is attributed to the fact that while the Qur'ãnic exhortations for the study of science were taken very seriously by the early Muslims, the same were neglected by their later brethren. Prof. Abdul Ali further maintains that the Islamic intellectual heritage remains one of the neglected areas of research in the discipline of Islamic Studies. He, therefore draws the attention of devoted specialists on the subject to make a systematic study of the intellectual and scientific contributions of Islam and Muslims in different branches of knowledge, particularly natural and exact sciences.

The above account is followed by a brief introduction to the major achievements of Muslim scientists in some of the important natural and exact sciences, namely medicine, surgery, anatomy, psychotherapy, zoology and veterinary medicine, botany and agriculture, mathematics, trigonometry, astronomy, etc.

Lastly, this address closes with due stress on the point that the promotion of studies and research on scientific foundations of Islam as well as on contributions of Muslim scientists will not only give them their proper place in the history of science and civilization, but also present to the modern people the genuine image of Islam as a mission for the welfare of humanity at large.

The sixth Presidential Address presented at the Arabic and Persian Section of the 37th Session of the A.I.O. Conference held at Rohtak (Haryana) in 1994, opens up new vistas of research in Arabic, Persian, and Islamic Studies by emphasizing the importance of the hitherto little-studied role played by the numerous post-Abbasid Arab and Persian dynasties in the advancement of science and civilization. It upholds that, contrary to popular view, there existed a high level of civilization in the Muslim world even after the fall of the Abbasid Caliphate in the thirteenth century, and that the numerous dynasties that sprang up on the ruins of the vast Abbasid Empire generously patronized and carried on the traditions of Arab-Islamic learning on a wide scale which must be taken into consideration while making an assessment of Muslim contributions to human thought and progress. And a comprehensive picture of the scientific and literary progress made under the Syro-Egyptian Mamluk Dynasty (1250-1517 A.D.) has been attempted here as a case study.

It has been clearly brought out in this address that very impressive and outstanding achievements were made by the scientists and scholars of this period in different branches of knowledge and learning such as medicine, anatomy, surgery, ophthalmology, veterinary science and animal husbandry, zoology, mathematics and astronomy, biographical and historical literature, geographical literature, etc. Prof. Dr. Abdul Ali says that it is worthy of mention in this context that the keen interest taken by the illiterate, hot-blooded Mamluk soldiers in the cultivation of knowledge and learning adequately reflects that they had been greatly inspired by the spirit of Islam to promote the cause of knowledge and learning in their domain.

The seventh Presidential Address was presented at the Islamic Studies Section of the 38th Session of the A.I.O. Conference held at Jadavpur University, Calcutta, on January 28-30, 1997. It focuses on the contributions made by Arab-Muslim scientists in the field of exact sciences with special reference to mathematics, algebra, geometry, trigonometry, astronomy and physics. The part played by Arab-Muslim scientists in developing these sciences has been dealt with in detail with sufficient illustrations and examples drawn from different sources.

While evaluating the works of Muslim scientists such as Muhammad Bin Musa al-Khwarizmi, Abdul Rahman al-Sufi, Nasir al-Din al-Tusi, al-Battani, Ali Bin Yusuf, al-Biruni, Ibn al-Haytham, etc., Prof. Abdul Ali has stressed the need for research into the unexplored works of these authors, holding that what has been done so far is only a small fraction of the vast available literature. He, therefore, consideres it highly desirable that the manuscripts scattered across the globe should be scientifically studied and edited by the application of the critical and comparative method. Another important point raised by him in this context is that organized efforts should be made to undertake a co-ordinated programme for translating major Arabic and Persian works on scientific subjects into other languages, particularly English, Urdu and Hindi for the benefit of the historians of science not acquainted with these source languages.

The eighth Presidential Address was delivered at the Islamic Studies Section of the 39th Session of the A.I.O. Conference held under the auspices of M.S. University, Vadodara, on October 13-15, 1998. It deals with some of the remaining important aspects of the transmission of varied Arabico-Persian and Islamic elements into the cultural heritage of Europe with particular reference to the role played by Arab-Islamic literary genres in the development of modern European literature, specially fiction literature.

After discussing in detail the main channels of transmission of Arab-Islamic thoughts and ideas into the West, Dr. Abdul Ali observes that there lies a fertile field for studies and research in this particular branch of Islamic Studies. An attempt has been made by him to make an objective assessment of the impact of the main Arabic works-the *Kalîlah wa Dimnah*, the Maqãmãt of Badî ʻal-Zamãn and al-Harîrî, *Risãlat al-Ghufrãn* by Abul ʻAlã al-Maʻarrî, the *Arabian Nights*, etc. on European literatures with special reference to the *Arabian Nights*, right from the thirteenth century to modern times.

It is to be noted that there lies a big scope for further research on the diffusion of innumerable Islamic elements into several other manifestations of the cultural life of the Europeans such as architecture, fine arts, industries, sanitation, cousine, poetical compositions, music, etc. It is suggested by Prof. Abdul Ali that there is a growing need to undertake comprehensive, comparative research works in these and similar unexplored areas of Arabic, Persian and Islamic Studies.

The ninth and last Presidential Address was presented at the South-East Asian Studies Section of the 40th Session of the All-India Oriental Conference held at the University of Madras, Chennai, on May 28-30, 2000. Prof. Abdul Ali introduces South-East Asia, saying that it has been a vital and fertile region for the intermingling and interaction of different historical factors and cultural currents from very ancient times, and that, despite all the ethnic, linguistic and cultural variations found in it, this vast area has been looked upon by its neighbours from time immemorial as a region in its own right, thanks mainly to the broad commonalities that have kept its peoples united across time.

Prof. Ali further points out that of all the major religio-cultural systems found in this region, Islam was the last to enter and establish itself in it. While emerging in the course of time as a great cultural and political force, it was not only greatly influenced, but also even considerably reformulated by the existing traditions of this region, namely Hindu, Buddhist and Confucian. He also maintains that the Muslims of this region have not got the same attention as their counterparts in West Asia got due to various reasons, and that the available Western sources of information are not at all reliable as they are vitiated by their misconceptions about this religion as well as by their own neo-colonialist interests. It is commendable that this paper embodies an analytical study of matters relating to Islam and Muslims in this region.

From the foregoing it is clear that, far from being monotonous surveys of works done in the respective disciplines, these Presidential Addresses by Prof. Ali are scholarly studies on the hitherto neglected or little-studied aspects of the Arab-Islamic intellectual and scientific heritage. It is hoped that this volume will prove useful to both students and scholars of Arab-Islamic Studies. The historians of science and civilization will also find it informative and interesting. I do hope that publication of this book will be widely appreciated both at home and abroad.

Prof. N. Akmal Ayyubi
Former Chairman,
Department of Islamic Studies
Aligarh Muslim University,
Aligarh (U.P.)

PRESIDENTIAL ADDRESS: WEST ASIAN STUDIES SECTION,
29th Session, A.I.O.C., Poona (1978)

Mr. President and fellow delegates,

I am extremely thankful to the All-India Oriental Conference for having elected me as President of the West Asian Studies Section. I deem it a rare privilege and honour to get an opportunity to address such a distinguished gathering of learned scholars who have assembled here from all over the country to carry on the literary and cultural traditions of this ancient land, whose contribution to the promotion of peace and understanding in the world as well as development of human thought can hardly be overestimated. While accepting the heavy responsibility of this high office, I am fully conscious of my limitations and short-comings, and it is only with your help and co-operation that I hope to prove worthy of the confidence you have reposed in me.

First of all permit me to throw some light on the contemporary West Asian scene with special reference to the conflict of interests of Big Powers in this region because of its unique strategic position and huge natural resources, in order to assess in some detail what role our country, having close strategic link with this area and enjoying traditional friendship with most of the oil-rich West Asian nations, can play in their common struggle for economic prosperity and freedom from colonial exploitation.

West Asia is that sensitive part of the world whose confines are washed by the five seas-the Mediterranean, Black, Caspian, Red, and the Arabian Seas. Geographically it refers to the Eastern Mediterranean area and Western or South-Western Asia. Politically it includes 12 states namely, Egypt, Arabia, Yemen, Kuwait, Oman, The United Arab Emirates, Iraq, Syria, Lebanon, Israel, Iran and Turkey. The cultural limits of West Asia extend to the adjacent territories of Libya, Tunisia, Algeria and Morocco in North Africa. This region, with the addition of some more countries, is also known as the Middle East.

It is important to note that until a quarter of century ago the importance of this area lay mainly in its strategic position as the main connecting-link between the East and the West. Situated at the junction of Asia, Africa and Europe, this area links the three continents both by landroutes and water-ways. The Mediterranean Sea, the Red Sea, the Arabian Sea, and later the Suez Canal, have through the ages rendered invaluable services to man in his communications, travels and trade. Even in the modern age of air travel and space technology these water-ways have not lost their age-old usefulness and value, simply because the largest volume of trade and raw materials is carried by ships and vessels. This is fully substantiated by the fact that the closure of the Suez Canal, following the Arab-Islraeli war in 1967, not only aroused great hue and cry in foreign offices of world Powers, but also it cost the oil-importing industrialised Western nations an additional amount of one thousand million dollars in a single year for carrying oil by supertankers via the Cape of Good Hope to their respective lands. The importance of the Suez Canal route has been expressed by Walter Fogg in the following words:-

"This arises from the inescapable geographical fact that for ships plying between ports of all the European countries as well as those of other Mediterranean lands, and those on the shores of the Indian Ocean and China Seas, there is no alternative water route other than the vastly more circuitous way round the the Cape of Good Hope. What this means in time and cost is illustrated by the following nautical mileages: London to Bombay via Suez 6200, via the Cape 10,700; Naples to Mombasa via

Suez 6500, via the Cape 8,900; Southampton to Abadan via Suez 4000, via the Cape 11,300."[1]

It is due to this excellent geographical position that this region has been, during the ancient periods of history, the common meeting ground of various nations. This is exactly the reason why the aspirants to mastery of the world, both ancient and modern, felt the necessity to control this region. For example the ancient Egyptians, the Babylonians and the Persians, conquered this area and controlled it during their heydays. And in our own days the Big Powers who have avoided war and confrontation in their home territories are engaged in a desperate struggle for gaining spheres of influence and bases of strategic value in this region not only to exploit its natural resources but also to take advantage of its strategic position in case a third World War breaks out between the two hostile blocs, the Capitalist West and the Communist East.

In short the unique strategic position of this region has exerted a powerful influence on the history of mankind since the earliest recorded times and for this reason alone this area shall always remain of vital importance to all the nations of the world, even if its natural resources are exhausted.

Another potent factor which has made this region more significant in the eyes of the outside world is its huge natural resources, among which oil is the main item. Small oil-fields have been found in Turkey, Egypt, Syria and Israel, but the large ones are those of Iran & Iraq and those along the Persian Gulf in Saudi Arabia, Kuwait and the United Arab Emirates. The fact that the known reserves of the West Asian oil are much greater than those of any oil-producing region has greatly increased the world importance of this area in the eyes of the Big Powers.

---

1. The Changing Map of Asia edited by W. Gordon & O.H.K. Spate, PP. 116-117.

In addition to oil this region is rich in iron-ore, phosphate, sulphur, natural gas, potassium, magnesium and other minerals. For instance the Arab production of phosphate constitutes more than 20% of the world production and the Arab countries produced 40% of world exports of phosphate in 1975.

Besides its strategic importance and rich natural resources, the West Asian region provides a vast market to industrialized Big Powers for their technology, weapons, skilled labour and industrial products, because these countries which have recently emerged as independent nations are industrially backward and therefore they have to depend on technically advanced nations for their technological help to industrialise themselves.

All these factors are jointly responsible for the conflict of interests of Big Powers resulting into an intense power rivalry in this region. And it is in the light of this fact that the West Asian crisis must be seen for a proper understanding of this problem.

Besides, in recent years some major developments have taken place in this area which cannot be ignored for an adequate understanding of the West Asian politics. Some of them are given below:—

1. The Petroleum-exporting West Asian nations have become enormously rich as a result of steep rise in oil prices during the last five years. As is well-known, when the Arabs imposed an embargo on oil supplies to the U.S.A. and other supporters of Israel, following the 1973 Arab-Israeli war, it caused wide-spread energy shortages and speeded up an economic recession in the West. At the same time they raised the price of petrol four-fold in one dramatic move. Not being satisfied with this much of rise in the price of oil, they repeatedly enhanced it afterwards in such a manner that it has by now increased something like six-fold in the last five years. This phenomenal enrichment of these nations has resulted into an

increasingly important role for them in world politics and economics. And in the near future the West Asian oil, mainly the Arab oil, is likely to play a more vital role in world politics because of the substantial dependence on it of the U.S.A., Japan and Western Europe by mid-1980s- each of them would be importing around six million barrels a day, according to a recent annual report of the Organization of the Arab Petroleum-Exporting Countries. By virtue of this economic leverage acquired by them through petro-dollars they are now in a position to play a major role in formulating a new international economic system enabling the developing countries of the third world to promote their industrial and other economic sectors.

2. With vast funds in their coffers these nations have launched on massive industrialisation of their lands in order to survive economically after their oil resources are exhausted. To achieve this they have to depend on the technology and industrial products of the Western nations. But these nations are very shrewd and they have increased the prices of their manufactured goods more than those of oil. Thus what they give out with one hand in higher oil prices they take back with the other in increased prices of their own goods and weapons. With this end in view the Western Companies exaggerated and over-priced their cost-estimates for the development projects in this region. But in some cases when they were exposed, their offers were cancelled. For example the offers made by G.E.C. Overseas Services, Belfour Bealty and Hawker Siddeley of the U.K., Siemens A.G. and MAN of West Germany and Brown Boveri of Switzerland were cancelled after Saudi Arabia discovered that their bids were overpriced. This is one of the main reasons why the West Asian nations have now started 'looking eastward' for technological help and skilled labour instead of solely

depending on the Western nations, who have been mercilessly exploiting them and their natural resources for the last two centuries. As a result of this development the friendly West Asian nations are now looking forward with high expectations to India's significant role in their diversified development projects because of the tremendous strides made by her in the industrial and technological fields including nuclear and space science and also because of the traditional friendship which has existed between them since the earliest recorded times. The big contracts which India has won in these countries as well as the large number of economic and technical exchanges that have taken place in recent years are a clear indication of this fact. But this development is so much resented by the Western nations that they are busy misrepresenting India's position in that region.

3. Another important point to be noted in this connection is that the Big Powers, mainly the two Super Powers the United States and the Soviet Union are determined to exploit this region at all cost. Apparently they are making all possible efforts to win the good-will of the local population by making false assurances of doing justice to them and also by seeking to appreciate their culture and civilization. In the face of this fact the possibility of the petro-dollars having been one of the main motives behind the historic world festival of Islam organised in London by the West in 1976 cannot be entirely ruled out. But inwardly the Super Powers seem to be in agreement with each other to a certain degree at least on one point, i.e., to keep the oil-rich West Asian region politically divided and technologically backward so that they may remain helpless puppets in their hands and the latter may continue to exploit the wealth of this region by weakening mainly the Arabs, the dominant element in the population of West Asia. To achieve this they want to maintain tension in this area. It is with this end in view that

they supply their West Asian proteges with lethal weapons always keeping the balance of power in favour of Israel, so that they may fight one another and thus weaken themselves. And the creation of the Jewish State of Israel in the heart of the Arab world by the Big Powers and their continuing support to its aggressive expansionist policy is a clear proof of their bad intention on this oil-rich area of strategic importance.

These and other developments taking place in West Asia deserve to be carefully watched and studied by the makers of India's foreign policy. Because for a number of reasons this country cannot remain unaffected by and immune to the evolving problems of this area. They may be described as strategic, political and economic.

Strategically, the West Asian region is of vital importance to India not only because her route to Europe lies through it but also because there is a direct link between the Mediterranean Sea and the Indian Ocean with the result that whenever the current power rivalry in West Asia or in the near-by area assumes a serious turn, it is fully reflected in the Indian Ocean also. For example when the Somali-Ethiopean conflict in the Horn of Africa took a serious turn in February 1978, America reacted by making a show of its naval force in the Indian Ocean. This undoubtedly created much tension in this area, due to which the Government of India wrote to both President Carter of America and President Brezhnev of Russia urging restraint and the need to avoid a situation in which the area might become a centre of Big Power conflict.

In view of this strategic link between the Indian Ocean and the oil-rich West Asian region it is not difficult to understand why the two Super Powers are competing with each other in maintaining military bases in the Ocean. In this connection it may be mentioned that the U.S.A. has already constructed a good number of bases in the eastern and western coasts of the Ocean, of which the Diego Garcia base is the most important because of its central location. Similarly the Russian navy normally maintains 20 or more ships in the Indian Ocean and has recently concentrated its vessels in the Red Sea and the Gulf of Aden lending military support to Ethiopia. Thus the presence of the large number of foreign fleets and naval task forces in the Indian Ocean poses a real hazard not only to the security of the West Asian nations but also to the security of the African and Asian countries along the Indian Ocean. It is mainly under this tension that the littoral states have been demanding time and again that the Indian Ocean should be declared as a zone of peace. But remember, my friends, that all their demands and cries to keep the Indian Ocean free from foreign military presence are doomed to fall on deaf ears unless the affected countries of Asia and Africa are united together and emerge into a Power to match up to the challenging situation, having knowledge of the fact that the elimination of tension in the Indian Ocean depends to a great extent on the elimination of power rivalry in West Asia.

From the political and cultural point of view there has been a long and traditional friendship between India and the West Asian peoples, mainly the Arabs and the Persians. Today India is a good friend of the Arabs. On international issues both the Indians and the Arabs seem to have identical views. Our country has been giving full support to them in their just struggle for vacation of their territories occupied by Israel. The chief characteristic of the current Indo-Arab friendship is that it is not based on the shaky foundation of diplomatic campaigns and political adjustments motivated by self-interest in the arena of International Politics, but rather it is the result of ever-strengthening cultural ties between the two sides through the ages.

Another important feature of the Indo-Arab friendship lies in the fact that instead of being confined to the rulers and diplomats of these people, it has been felt and expressed by their poets and masses also. This is fully corroborated by the warm welcome which was accorded to Mahatma Gandhi by the Egyptians when he passed through Egypt in 1931 on his way to London to participate at the Second Round Table Conference as a delegate of the Indian National Congress for discussion on the future constitutional set-up of India.

On this occasion Ahmad Shawqi, a famous Arabic Poet composed an Ode in honour of Mahatma Gandhi. In order to give you an idea of the support and sympathy which the Arabs extended to the Indians in their struggle for freedom from the British yoke, the verses of the Ode are translated below:—

> O Sons of Egypt! Raise your garlands and greet the hero of India,
>
> And perform your duty and fulfil the rights of this matchless leader.
>
> He is your brother in enduring hardship and in facing the difficult situation.
>
> And in offering the greatest sacrifice; and in the demand and struggle (for freedom),
>
> And in being wounded, in shedding tears, and in being sent into exile from the cradle,
>
> And in the journey for truth and at the stage of delegation.
>
> Stand and salute 'the hero on the ship' from near and far;
>
> And cover the land with myrtle and the sea with rose-flowers.

• • • • •

> Upon the frieze of the Rajputana (the ship) there stands a statue of glory;
>
> He appears to be a prophet like Confucius or something of that type,
>
> In speech and action he is very much like the awaited Messiah,
>
> In piety and in the defence of truth he resembles the Apostles;
>
> Certainly he has preached truth, patience and moderation;

And when he called the Far East, it responded to him from the grave.

And he came to the sick souls and cured them of malice.

He invited the Hindus and the Muslims for unity and mutual love.

And he gathered the two swords (i.e., the Hindus and the Muslims) in one and the same sheath by the magic of his spiritual power,

And by the power of his soul which gives strength to the 'tamers of the lion',

And by the divine guidance which he receives from God and by the prosperity of his good fortune,

And by his good luck which is not granted except to the one created for immortality;

And he is not over-powered by the might, attack and army (of the enemy),

And neither does he get affected by the consideration of race and wealth, nor by fatigue and hard work,

And it is nothing but the gift of Almighty God for the servant.

• • • • •

O Gandhi! Accept the greetings of the Nile; and accept this flower on my behalf,

And be honoured on behalf of the Pyramids and the date-trees,

And on behalf of the Shaikhs of the Valley as well as its beardless cubs.

We all salute you over and over again, O milker of the cattle and spinner at the spindle!

And who avoids the use of salt and does not incline towards honey,

And who walks on foot from Hind to Sind.

We all salute you whenever you offer your prayers half-naked in the loin-cloth,
And in the cell of the prison as well as in the chains of arrest.

• • • • •

O Gandhi! Beware of the Green Table—i.e., the Round Table Conference,
And carefully observe the faces of the 'Sirs' and the 'Lords';
And be the most skilful of the players at the Chess and the Backgammon,
And meet the Lords as an equal meets his equal;
And say: Bring your snakes, for the snake-charmer has come from India,
And don't care for the accuser, nor get deceived by the praise,
For no criticism can aspire to approach this star;
And return India to the nation from border to border.

• • • • •

Besides, India has a larger Muslim population than any of the West Asian Muslim nations. This also has been one of the main factors which led to the strengthening of cultural and political contacts between the two sides. Here it is worth mentioning that because of the long and close association of the Arabs and the Persians with the Indians, there has been a lively intellectual and cultural interchange between what these peoples possessed in different branches of knowledge and learning. And the rich cultivation of Arabic and Persian studies in the country gave birth to a large number of eminent Arabic and Persian scholars, of whom India shall always remain proud in the midst of the Muslim countries of the world. They not only preserved and carried on the traditions of Arabic, Persian and Islamic studies in this country, but also contributed a great deal to the mainstream of Indian culture. These close political and cultural contacts between the two sides have all the more brightened the prospects of India's participation on a wide scale in the industrial and technological development of the West Asian nations on mutually beneficial terms.

And lastly as regards India's economic interests, West Asia holds no less attraction for this country than it has for the Big Powers. It is one of the best customers of our products, both industrial and consumer goods. India exports to these countries sugar, tea, meat, electric and non-electric machinery, manufactures of metals, jute products, transport equipment and other varieties of machinery earning thereby billions of foreign exchange which has undoubtedly played a significant role in making our country economically strong and technologically developed. In recent years there has been a spurt in the export of non-traditional items, particularly engineering goods, chemicals and steel products. This has led to tremendous increase in India's total exports to West Asian countries. For example in 1973-74 our exports to these countries amounted to Rs. 17, 79 million only which increased nearly four-fold to Rs. 7036 million in 1976-77.

In recent years India has also won a large number of contracts for various development projects in West Asia. Some of the major projects for which contracts were won are: an integrated modern township in Kuwait of the value of $270 million; a large power project worth $130 million and construction of an airport costing Rs. 360 million in Libya; a housing complex in Dubai worth $64 million; a power generation plant costing Rs. 100 core in Saudi Arabia and a $12 million contract for the Hindustan Machine Tools to assist in the production of water and gas meters and gas regulators in Algeria.

Besides, a large number of Indian doctors, engineers, teachers, economists, development experts and workers, both skilled and unskilled, are working in all the friendly West Asian nations. According to an official report, at present about one million Indians are serving in these countries, whose annual remittances total more than Rs. 2000 crore.

Of the other sources through which we get huge amounts of foreign exchange from this region, mention may be made of Tourism, Film and Book industries. Our university level text-books are exported on a large scale to these countries and are prescribed in their university courses. Our films are also very popular there which not only earn foreign exchange but also act as a kind of cultural ambassador in those lands. And as regards tourism industry, it is gratifying to note that our country has started attracting a large number of tourists from this region where the hike in petroleum prices has enabled people to travel and spend more money abroad. And the new air services and tourist information centres which have been opened in several West Asian countries have undoubtedly boosted this industry by helping to create an awareness of what India offers to tourists.

But considering the vast and growing potential of this region for economic development, whatever India has achieved so far can only be described as a modest beginning, and in view of the deep understanding and close political and cultural relations between the two sides, there is still a big scope for further economic collaboration and trade between them. Thus by proper efforts our country can best serve the vast market for technology, services, manpower and goods that has opened up in all the oil-rich West Asian nations. But to achieve this objective effectively she must not only project her industrial image in that area but also she must further strengthen her political and cultural contacts with them by keeping herself fully acquainted with their culture, thoughts, habits and modern outlook, because "to win the Middle East," as has been observed by S.N. Fisher, an American scholar, "requires the winning of the Middle Eastern peoples. Like a rich girl the people of the Middle East do not want to be wooed for wealthy oil possessions or valuable real estate. They wish to be courted for themselves. Their culture, skills and civilization must be understood and appreciated and their desires respected.[1]" At the

1. S.N. Fisher: Middle East-A History, P. 749.

same time it is also quite advisable that our country should give more active support to them in their struggle to get rid of the remaining vestiges of Western Imperialism, because it will not only serve our national interests, but also it will be in complete consonance with our foreign policy of giving support to other countries on the basis of the principles of justice and truth.

In the light of the points discussed above it is quite clear that there is a growing need for the promotion of studies and research in West Asian history, politics, economics, sociology and culture. In this connection it is worthy of notice that the Department of West Asian Studies at Jawahar Lal Nehru University, Delhi, and the Centre of West Asian Studies at Aligarh Muslim University are doing commendable work in studies and research on West Asian subjects. They have published a number of theses and research papers throwing light on the political and economic developments in West Asia. Besides, some good books also have been published. Of them mention may be made of 'Communism in the Arab East, 'the Lebanese Crisis,' and 'Politics in the Gulf' by Dr. M.S. Agwani, Professor of West Asian Studies, Jawahar Lal Nehru University, Delhi, and 'Anwar al Sadat' and 'Consequences of the October War' by Col. B.K. Narayan. These books provide deep insights into the social, political, economic and military developments in the region in the context of the manipulations of the Big Powers to strengthen their hold on this strategic part of the world.

But considering the vastness of the field of West Asian Studies it is highly desirable and imperative that some more universities should be encouraged to start centres of West Asian Studies where proper emphasis should be put on the need to understand the modern thinkers and writers of West Asia in original rather than through the writings of Western scholars whose interpretations are but naturally coloured by their imperialistic motives.

Lastly, I thank you once again for the honour you have done me and patient hearing you have so kindly given to me.

PRESIDENTIAL ADDRESS: ARABIC & PERSIAN SECTION
31st Session, A.I.O.C., Jaipur (1982)

Mr. President, Distinguished Delegates and Friends,

I am extremely thankful to the authorities of the All-India Oriental Conference for having elected me as President of the Arabic & Persian Section of the 31st Session of the Conference that is being held at this historic city of Jaipur. While accepting the heavy responsibility of this high office, I am fully conscious of my limitations and shortcomings, and it is only with your help and co-operation that I hope to prove worthy of the confidence you have reposed in me.

At the very outset I would like to make a brief assessment of the part played by Arabic and Persian languages in the advancement of human knowledge and learning as well as of their contributions to the cultural heritage of India.

It is a well-known fact that with the rise of Islam the Arabs became united and emerged as a powerful nation. And within a century after their rise they became the masters of a vast empire which extended from the shores of the Atlantic Ocean to the confines of China, an empire greater than that of Rome at its zenith.

It was not only an empire which the Arabs built but also a culture. Inspired by the Verses of the Qur'ãn and Traditions of Prophet Muhammad and filled with the spirit of scientific enquiry, they travelled far and wide in search of knowledge, and contributed a great deal to human thought and progress. Arabic soon became the language of natural sciences, medicine and philosophy. And between the beginning of the eighth and the middle of the thirteenth centuries the Arabic-speaking peoples were the main bearers of the torch of culture and civilization throughout the world, while Arabic translations were the instrument whereby the ancient sciences and intellectual legacies of Greece, Iran and India were preserved, supplemented and transmitted to the West, which made possible the renaissance of Western Europe. This was the golden period of Arab history. It was also the period of Persian ascendancy and cosmopolitan culture. Baghdad, the wonderful Abbasid capital, was built on Persian soil, while Persian nobles filled the highest offices of state at the Abbasid court.

Here it should be remembered that had the Arabs done nothing apart from saving and preserving the ancient sciences of the then civilized world, even then they would deserve the appreciation of the twentieth century scholars for this reason alone, for preservation and transmission of knowledge from the standpoint of the history of culture, is no less important than making original contributions. Otherwise, as P.K. Hitti has put it "Had the researches of Aristotle, Galen and Ptolemy been lost to posterity, the world would have been as poor as if they had never been produced."

In short, it can be rightly said that history does not know any other nation which has contributed so much in a comparatively brief span of time as did the Arabs and Arabic-speaking peoples. The famous Muslim capitals like Cairo, Damascus, Baghdad and Cordova etc., became the chief centres of spreading education and conducing scientific researches. An idea of their contribution to human thought and progress can be easily gained from the fact that when misfortunes befell the Muslim world in general and the Arabs of Spain, France and Italy in particular, the most precious booty treasured by the Europeans was a large number of valuable Arabic books and manuscripts. Prof. Umar al-Dasuqi has mentioned in his book titled *Fil-Adab-il-Hadith* that the Europeans collected more than 2,50,000 rare Arabic books and manuscripts, and decorated their libraries with them. For example, the libraries of Berlin, Paris, London, Leipzig, Leiden, Oxford and Madrid etc., are still very famous for having a large number of rare Arabic books and manuscripts on different branches of learning cultivated by the Arabic-speaking peoples.

The Arabs made valuable contributions, especially in historical, geographical, philosophical, mathematical and medical studies. Although here it is not possible to enter into details of their achievements in these fields, a passing reference to a few outstanding scholars who wrote in Arabic may appropriately be made in this connection. For example, Ibn Khaldun, the greatest historical thinker of Islam, is admired in the West as founder of the modern sciences of sociology and historiography. And as R.A. Nicholson has observed, "His intellectual descendants ere the great medieval and modern historians of Europe-Machiavelli and Vico and Gibbon." In the realm of geography the names of Ibn Khurdadhbih, Ibn Hawqal, Yaqut, al-Bakri and al-Idrisi are very famous. The great mathematician, al-Khwarizmi, wrote the oldest work on algebra with over eight hundred examples known as *Hisab-ul-Jabr w-al-Muqabalah* (the calculation of integration and equation). It is remarkable to note that the Latin version of this book was used until the sixteenth century as the main mathematical text-book by western scholars. Of the original writers on medicine Ibn Zakariya al-Razi, the author of *al-Hawi*, an encyclopaedia on medicine; Ibn Sina, the author of the *Canon of Medicine*; and Abul Qasim al-Zahrawi, the greatest Arab surgeon of medieval times, are very famous. Upto the sixteenth century the works of these authors constituted the basis of the lectures on medicine in European universities. Similarly, the Arab contributions to the development of philosophical studies can be judged from the fact that Muslim philosophy continued to be taught in the universities of Europe upto the middle of the seventeenth century, and that Aristotle was understood in the West only through the commentaries of Ibn Rushd for a long time. Besides, they achieved considerable distinction in Chemistry, Mineralogy, Botany, Fine Arts and Music, etc. Their contributions to these fields of knowledge form the connecting link between the Graeco-Roman classical age and the modern civilization. In view of this fact they can justifiably be called as harbingers of the modern scientific age. An idea of the importance of Arabic as depository of scientific knowledge can be derived from what Becker, a German scientist used to say: "The contribution of the Arabs to science is so important that if I knew I have still 20 years to live and that I could get an abundant supply of Arabic books on science, I would learn Arabic even at this advanced stage of my life." Their contribution to modern civilization is further acknowledged by Briffault in his *Making of Humanity* in the following words: "What we call science arose in Europe as a result of a new spirit of enquiry, of new methods of investigation, of the method of experiment, observation, measurement, of the development of mathematics in a form unknown to the Greeks. That spirit and those methods were introduced into the European world by the Arabs."

Similarly, the contribution of Persian language to the advancement of human knowledge and civilization can hardly be overestimated. It is common knowledge that after the destruction of the Abbasid Caliphate at the hands of the Mongols, Arabic began to lose rapidly the proud status of being the lingua franca of the Muslim world, and was gradually replaced by local languages, especially Persian and Turkish. The Persians had already, even before the collapse of the Abbasid Caliphate, begun the experiment of producing scientific works in their language. For instance, Ibn Sina wrote his *Danish Nama-e-Alai* in Persian, although his major works were written in Arabic.

Again, Persian was not confined to Iran alone. It spread with the Muslim conquests to India also where Arabic enjoyed at best a religious importance only. The Saljuqs, although racially

Turks, were patrons of Persian language, literature and culture. Under them Persian flourished both in Persia and Anatolia as the language of culture and literature. The Ottoman Turks who supplanted the Saljuqs as the dominant power in West Asia also patronised Persian language and literature so much that cultured men vied with one another in writing Persian poetry. Sultan Salim I of Turkey, for instance, wrote Persian poetry and had a Persian Diwan to his credit. We also know that Persian continued to be a compulsory subject of study in Turkey till the replacement of the Arabic script by the Latin in 1928 under Mustafa Kamal. Thus Persian replaced Arabic in most of the Muslim lands as the language of both culture and religion.

Now coming to the contribution of Arabic and Persian to the cultural heritage of India, I would like to emphasize that both these languages have played such an important role in preserving and enriching the Indian culture that a correct appreciation of the history and cultural heritage of this country is not possible without the aid of Indo-Arab and Indo-Persian literatures.

Perhaps, the most significant contribution of Arabic to the cultural heritage of India lies in the fact that it was mostly through this language that the ancient intellectual legacy of this country was preserved, enriched and made known to the outside world. The names of al-Fazari, al-Kindi, al-Khwarizmi and al-Biruni etc., are well-known in history for bringing about a lively intellectual interchange between what the Indians and the Arabs possessed in different branches of knowledge and learning. In the field of mathematics and astronomy the Arabs first translated into Arabic *Siddhãnta*, a treatise on astronomy in Sanskrit, as a result of which a systematic study of the stars was undertaken by them. They also discovered and learned from this book the use of Indian numerals, which when introduced in Europe, brought about a revolution in the science of calculation.

It may also be claimed that the Arabs not only preserved and transmitted the Indian legacy, but also enriched it with fresh contributions of their own, as they did not come to India empty-handed. They brought with them a great deal of wisdom and skill which they had acquired from the Greeks. For instance, the influence of the Arabs on Indian astronomy may be assessed from the fact that the Indian astronomers took from them a number of technical terms, their methods of calculation of the latitudes and logitudes and in horoscopy a whole branch called *Tajik*.

While discussing the cultural give-and-take between India and the Arab world, we must not fail to pay our special attention to the above-mentioned Abu Rayhan al-Biruni, a renowned Arabist of Persian origin who stayed in India for several years, and acquainted himself with the language, philosophy and sciences of this country. He has given a very authentic account of the sciences, antiquities and customs of India in his famous book called *Tarikh-ul-Hind*. The celebrated German Orientalist E. Sachau has commented on the importance of this book by saying that the books written about India before al-Biruni are nothing but babies' toys in comparison with his book containing scientific researches.

Likewise, the contribution of Persian to the cultural heritage of India is all the more important. It has been the court-language of this sub-continent for about eight centuries, and it is deeply rooted in the life and composite culture of our country.

The close relation between the Persian and Indian cultures is too well-known to be recounted. Both the people of Persia and the Aryans of India are descendants of the same stock. There is so much affinity between the language of the Avesta and Sanskrit that oriental scholars of the old Iranian language find knowledge of Sanskrit of great help in their understanding of the Avesta.

Here it also may be recalled that when Babur came to India, he brought with him a Central Asian culture which was thoroughly

Persianized owing to the fact that the Mughals were closely associated with that country. Babur himself, being well-grounded in Persian language and culture, composed poetry in Persian. Besides, the cultural patterns of Islam too came to India through Persian channels. This process provided ample opportunities for Persian language and literature to lay their indelible marks on Indian languages and culture.

One great debt which India owes to Arabic and Persian is the fact that it was mainly through these languages that the ancient wisdom literature of this country was preserved and made known to the West. For example, the animal fables of Sanskrit origin, known as the fables of Bidpai were translated into Arabic by Ibn-ul-Muqaffa from Pahlavi under the title *Kalilah wa Dimnah*. What gives the Arabic version special significance is the fact that it became the basis of all existing translations into various European and Asian languages.

Again, as has been rightly described by Prof. S.A.H. Abidi in his presidential address delivered at the fourth session of the All-India Persian Teachers Conference, it was through Persian translation of the Upanishads by Dara Shikoh under the title *Sirr-i-Akbar* that the European orientalists became acquainted with and took keen interest in the study of our Vedic and Post-Vedic Sanskrit literature.

Another important aspect of the Indo-Arab and Indo-Persian literary, cultural and intellectual interchange is to be found in the rich cultivation of Arabic and Persian studies in India. There is no denying the fact that the growth of Islam in this country marks the emergence of a new epoch in the history of its cultural evolution. Education which so far had been confined to the privileged few was now made open to all. And the study of Arabic and Persian naturally occupied an important position in the educational curriculum of this country. As a result, it gave birth to a large number of Arabic and

Persian scholars, who not only carried on the traditions of Arabic and Persian learning in this country, but also enriched the Indo-Arab and Indo-Persian literature with valuable contributions of their own which cannot be ignored while making an assessment of the literary achievements of Indian authors. They wrote volumes of Arabic and Persian books on both secular and religious subjects. Of the notable Arabic writers mention may be made of the following of whom our country shall always remain proud in the midst of the Arab countries of the world:

Imam Hasan bin Muhammad is author of *al-Ubab-ul-Dhakhir*, *Majma-ul-Bahrayn* and *Kitab-ul-Addãd* on philology, and *Mashariq-ul-Anwar* on Hadith; Shaikh Ali bin Hishamuddin of Burhanpur, author of *Kanz-ul-Ummal;* Allamah Mahmud of Jawnpur, author of *al-Faraid fi Ulum-il-Balaghah;* Muhibbullah al-Bihari, author of *Musallam-ul-Thubut* on principles of Jurisprudence; Sayyid Murtada al-Bilgrami, author of *Taj-ul-Arus fi Sharh-îl-Qamus*; Nawab Siddiq Hasan Khan of Bhopal, author of 222 books in Arabic, Persian and Urdu; and Shaikh Abdul Hayy of Lucknow, author of 110 books including 86 books in Arabic on various subjects of Arabic and Islamic studies.

In the realm of Persian Amir Khusrau, Abul Fayd Faydi, Dara Shikoh, Asadullah Khan Ghalib and Allamah Muhammad Iqbal, to mention only a few names out of a legion, are very famous, It is a matter of pride for our country that the Indian style of Persian known to fame as *Sabk-e-Hindi* was duly recognised and appreciated in the Persian-speaking world.

But it is a matter of great pity that the works of the above and other eminent Indian authors in these languages, though quite popular abroad, have not received sufficient attention of our scholars. So Arabic and Persian works produced in our country seem to be a neglected area of research. It is now high time that scholars pursuing Arabic and Persian researches should undertake, without further loss of time, a systematic and comprehensive study of these authors and their works, so that their contributions may be critically assessed and their achievements appreciated.

Besides, a good number of Arabic and Persian books and manuscripts bearing on Indian history, geography and culture await the attention of our scholars. Research and investigation in this field are not only likely to be immensely rewarding, but also they will help to present a correct picture of history and culture. Such books should also be translated into major Indian languages for the benefit of our fellow brothers who are not acquainted with Arabic and Persian.

In his presidential address titled *India and the Arab World through the Ages* delivered at the 38th session of the Indian History Codgress, Prof. M.S. Khan, while emphasising the need for making a detailed, critical and well-documented study of the history of the Indo-Arab relations, has made a survey and evaluation of the work already done on the subject which I need not repeat here. But I shall simply point out by way of illustration that Arabic literature bearing on Indian history contains a very good image of our legacy and country. Arab travellers right from merchant Sulaiman of the ninth century to Ibn Battutah of the fourteenth display the admiration, love and affection of the Arabs for this country and its people.

While talking of the traditions of Arabic and Persian studies as carried on in our country in the past, I cannot remain without referring to unsatisfactory conditions of teaching and learning in these subjects at present, It is no longer a secret that our modern colleges and universities have failed to provide, barring a few exceptions, the type of scholars who can hand down the true Arabic and Persian learning. In case of Arabic, for instance, the standards of learning at the Indian universities have so much deteriotated in recent years that most of our M.A., and Doctorate degrees holders are not able to read, write and speak even simple Arabic, leave apart their ability to be well-grounded in the subject. Indeed it is sad to note that our universities have not been able to produce the expertise needed by our nation for international communication in this language. But now we cannot afford to permit this state of affairs to continue for a long time. It is, therefore, high time for us that we should reorient and restructure our courses so as to make university education in these subjects more fruitful and more in tune with our national interests.

A word of praise must be expressed here for some of our traditional Madrasahs and Seminaries imparting instruction in Arabic, specially Nadwat-ul-Ulama at Lucknow, whose products become comparatively better skilled in the use of this language. The Department of Arabic at the Central Institute of English and Foreign Languages, Hyderabad, also deserves our appreciation for making satisfactory progress in this particular direction under the headship of Prof. Abdul Halim Nadwi. It is worthy of mention in this context that recently an All-India Arabic Seminar was held under the auspices of the CIEFL on "THE PROBLEMS OF TEACHING ARABIC IN INDIA WITH SPECIAL FOCUS ON SYLLABUS, AIMS AND METHODS, which was inaugurated by Sayyid Abul Hasan Ali al-Nadwi, Rector of Nadwat-ul-Ulama, Lucknow. One important feature of this Seminar was that its proceedings were conducted in Arabic and also that majority of the delegates presented their papers in the same language. Such seminars should be frequently held in both Arabic and Persian as they provide forums for discussing problems connected with studies and research in these subjects.

I shall make a few more suggestions for our general guidance. First, preparation of general descriptive catalogues of the various Arabic and Persian manuscripts which are lying scattered all over the world is urgently needed. Non-availability of such catalogues not only renders the work of research tedious and difficult, but also keeps the research scholars in the dark about some of the available source materials in their respective fields of studies. It is, therefore, suggested that publication of a general descriptive catalogue should be undertaken by scholars on a priority basis. Obviously, this work cannot be done except through co-operation and co-ordination of research centres all over the world. Completion of this work is sure to give great impetus to research and the consequent enhancement of knowledge.

Publication of unpublished texts and manuscripts in these languages is yet another important work which requires our immediate attention. As estimated by Arab scholars and experts, there are about one million manuscripts in Arabic alone. Perhaps, this is the largest number of manuscripts which any single language can claim to its credit. Out of this vast number about 9 lakh manuscripts still await analysis and publication. This is a matter of considerable urgency, otherwise some of these valuable materials might soon perish for want of proper care and custody. If these along with the numerous Persian manuscripts are published, they are bound to throw flood-light on the hitherto unknown aspects of the legacies of Arabic and Persian.

Similarly, publication of systematic and regular research bulletins giving information regarding the various research works being carried on at research centres all over the world will solve a great academic purpose. This will avoid much of duplication in research as well as wastage of precious intellectual energy which might otherwise be applied to explore and analyze other untouched sources of knowledge. It is worthy of mention in this context that the regular publication of the periodic Journal AL-LISAN-UL-ARABI by the Bureau of Co-ordination of Arabization at Rabat, Morocco, under the directorship of Prof. Abdul Aziz Benabdellah, has been greatly satisfying the needs of our research scholars. It enlightens them not only on researches on Arabic linguistic sciences, but also on the various aspects of research being carried on in the field of Arabic studies in general.

Last but not the least, introduction of inter-disciplinary courses in Arabic, Persian, Pali, Prakrit and other Indian languages on the basis of applied linguistics at some selected universities is also highly desirable and imperative. This will not only facilitate Indological studies on scientific lines, but also promote our national integration and communal harmony by pinpointing the various cultural cross-currents that constitute the composite culture of India. It is gratifying to note that the School of Comparative Languages and Culture at Bhopal University in Madhya Pradesh has already started offering such courses under the guidance of Dr. Hiralal Shukla, whose *Word Atlas of Baghelkhand* running into 2000 pages has been hailed in the academic world as a most pioneering work in the field of Indian linguistics. It is hoped that the various courses introduced by this School will not end up as mere repetitions of traditional courses, but rather it will set a good model for other centres of Indological studies to follow.

Finally, I thank you once again for the honour you have done me and patient hearing you have so kindly accorded to me.

PRESIDENTIAL ADDRESS: ISLAMIC STUDIES SECTION,
32nd Session, A.I.O.C., Ahmedabad (1985)

Distinguished Scholars, Ladies and Gentlemen,

Let me begin my address by expressing my sincere thanks to the authorities of the All-India Orietal Conference for giving me the opportunity to preside over the Islamic Studies Section of the 32nd session of the Conference being held under the auspices of the University of Gujarat at Ahmedabad.

Now permit me to draw your attention to the need for making a critical reassessment of the mentality and legacy of the pre-Islamic Arabs with a view to presenting a realistic and balanced image of them, rather than condemning them outright as a totally immoral, vicious and foolish lot. Needless to say that this will enable us to understand in a better manner not only the type of stuff they constituted for the rise and growth of Islam, but also the subsequent development of its various institutions.

It is a well-known fact that the Arabian Peninsula has been the cradle of the Semitic race. It is said to have nursed those peoples who later migrated into the Fertile Crescent and subsequently became the Babylonians, the Assyrians, the Phoenicians and the Hebrews. But it is unfortunate that of all the ancient peoples the pre-Islamic Arabs seem to have been the most grossly misrepresented by both Orientalists and Arab scholars.

It is true that the pre-Islamic Arabs, especially the northern Arabians, were a nomadic and haughty people. They lived mostly as wanderers from place to place in search of water and pasturage.

They had no settled government. It is also said that they remained confined to the peninsular deserts, and that they never came into contact with the civilized nations of the world.

They were full of vanity. They prided themselves on raiding and plundering their enemy tribes. To them blood called for blood. No punishment other than that of vengeance was acceptable to them. Their inter-tribal hostilities known as *Ayyãm al-'Arab* generally arose from disputes over cattle, pasture lands or springs. In some cases they lasted for a very long time. For example, the Basûs War between the Banû Bakr and the Banû Taghlib lasted for as many as forty years.

They also paid boundless and unconditional loyalty to their tribe under all circumstances. They supported their tribesmen in all matter irrespective of the fact whether they were right or wrong. This tribal zeal is elaborately expressed by the pre-Islamic poet Durayd b. Simmah in the following lines:

" هل انا الاّ من غزيّة ان غوت
غويتُ وان ترشد غزية أرشد "

(I am naught but a member of the Ghazîyah tribe.
If it goes astray, I shall also go astray; and if it
goes aright, I shall also go aright).[1]

Besides, they worshipped idols, drank wine, committed fornication and practised immorality of various sorts. Some tribes even buried their daughters alive in order to escape the responsibility of bringing them up. The Qur'ãn has referred to this in the following words:

" لاتقتلوا اولادكم خشية إملاق ... "

(Do not slaughter your children due to fear of poverty).[2]

There is no denying the fact that all these vices were rampant among the pre-Islamic Arabs. This has been adequately described by both Orientalists and Arab historians. But this is only one side of the coin. Like all other peoples the ancient Arabs also had some virtuous and good qualities which, unfortunately, have not been given their due importance by historians.

It is sad to note that while seeking to emphasize the importance of Islam in transforming the life of the pre-Islamic Arabs, even prominent Arab scholars such as Ibn Khaldûn, Muhammad 'Abdûh, 'Abbãs Mahmûd al-'Aqqãd and Muhammad Hasan al-Bãqûrî, etc., have painted them in the blackest of colours.[3] They have gone to the extreme ends in exaggerating their vices in gross neglect of the fact that they had some virtues, good qualities and positive points also. Thus they have done gross injustice to their ancestors by throwing light only on the negative side of their life. The impression one gets from their accounts of this people is that they were a wretched, misguided, idolatrous and despised people, that they were a foolish lot who saw no value whatsoever in intellect and knowledge, and also that they were morally and intellectually bankrupt. Consider, for example, the following quotations:

"انّ حملة العرب كانوا اهل بغى وإلحاد و قطع للأرحام، وتنافس فى الردى ، و اعراض عن ذكر اللّٰه ، فكانت عبادتهم الأوثان والحجارة ، و أكلهم العقارب والخنافس والحيات والجعلان ... " (ابن خلدون) -

> (The Arabs in general were a people of tyranny and heterodoxy. They severed their ties of kinship, and strove for death and perdition. They deviated from the worship of Allah, worshipped idols and stones, and fed on scorpions, buprestes, snakes and blackbeetles).[4]

"قد بلغ العرب من سخافة العقل حدا اصنعوا فيه أصنامهم من الحلوى ثم عبدوها، فلما جاعوا أكلوها، و بلغوا من تضعضع الأخلاق وهنا قتلوا فيه بناتهم تخلصا من عار حياتهن اوتنصلا من نفقات معيشتهن و بلغ الفحش فيه مبلغا لم يعد معه للعفاف قيمة ـ" (محمد عبده) ـ

(The Arabs were so week-minded and foolish that they made their idols out of sweetmeats and worshipped them. But when they felt hungry, they ate them. And morally, they had become so depraved that they slaughtered their daughters to get rid of (what they considered) the disgrace of their life as well as to be saved the responsibility of bringing them up. Immorality had become so rife among them that chastity was of no value to them).[5]

"عاشت امة جاهلية فكانت فى جملتها أذل الناس دلا ،و اشقاهم عيشا، وابينهم ضلالة ، واعراهم جلودا واجوعهم بطونا ... حتى جاء القرآن فنقلهم من الذلة الى العزة ، و من الشقاء الى السعادة ـ" (محمد حسن الباقورى) ـ

(The Arabs were an ignorant people. They were the most contemptible, the most wretched, the most misguided, the most naked (shameless) and the most hungry of all the peoples of the world. But when Islam came, it changed their baseness into glory and misery into prosperity).[6]

But a critical and objective study of their literary and linguistic heritage clearly reveals that, in spite of all the vices and faults that may be listed against them, at no stage of their history they had been morally and intellectually bankrupt. It is worthy of mention in this context that in Islamic parlance they were called *jãhil* (ignorant) not because of their stupidity or ignorance but because of their haughtiness and war-like attitude. An attempt has been made in this paper to throw light on some hitherto little-known aspects of the positive and constructive side of their life.

Contacts with Foreign Peoples

Far from remaining confined to the peninsular deserts, the pre-Islamic Arabs used to voyage fearlessly in the Arabian Gulf, the Red Sea and the India Ocean. They were the pioneers of maritime trade and acted as commercial intermediaries between the East and the West. They sailed on the Indian Ocean right upto the Pacific Sea and reached China. They had their permanent settlements on the western coast of India, in Ceylon, in Indo-China and China proper, which played a laudable role in spreading the message of Islam in different parts of the world.

The coast of Yemen was a great centre of maritime trade in the pre-Islamic period. It used to be crowded by Arab, Greek and Roman traders. The Arabs were in constant contact with Somalia, Ehtiopia, India and Iran. The port of Aden was an important centre for the exchange of commercial goods between India and Egypt. The presence of a large number of Greek and Roman traders in the city led to the foundation of a Christian church in it. This might have been one of the reasons responsible for the introduction of Christianity among the pre-Islamic Arabs.[7]

That the pre-Islamic Arabs were good navigators is further evidenced by such minute descriptions of the sea, the ships and their movement as are found in the pre-Islamic Arabic poetry. Take, for example, the following lines from the *mu'allaqah* (Ode) of the poet Tarafah, who lived in the third quarter of the sixth century A.D. in Bahrain on the eastern coast of the Peninsula. While comparing the camels' travelling to the tacking and sailing of ships, he says:

كأنّ حدوج المالكية غدوة
خلايا سفين بالنواصف من دد

عدولية او من سفين بن يامن
يجور بها الملاح طورا ويهتدى

يشق حباب الماء حيزومها بها
كما قسم الترب المفائل باليد

(As if the Malikian camels, with the howdahs, on the morning of her departure in the water-tracts of the village of Dad, were the big ships of Adoal, or the vessels of Ibn Yamin, which the sailors at times steer out of the straight course, and at times guide straight. Their bows cleave the ripple of the sea, as the divider of the sand-heaps separates the dust with his hand).[8]

The above lines clearly indicate that such minute description of the ship sailing on the sea would not have been possible for the poet, had he not experienced the voyage himself.

Another pre-Islamic poet and warrior, 'Amr b. Kulthûm boasts of his domination on land and sea in the following lines:

ملأنا البر حتّى ضاق عنّا
وظهر البحر نملأهٔ سفينا

(We have filled the land so that it has become narrow for us and have filled the sea with our boats).[9]

Besides, there are numerous Qur'ãnic references to the sea and its tempests. They not only give credence to early maritime activities of the Arabs, but also indicate that they were fully acquainted with the different situations of sailing in both normal and tempestuous conditions of these. This is clear from the following verses:

" ولـه الجوار المنشآت فى البحر كالأعلام "
(LV:24)

(His are the ships displayed upon the sea like mountains).[10]

" وترى الفلك مواخر فيه ولتبتغوا من فضله ولعلكم تشكرون "
(XVI:14)

(And thou seest the ships ploughing it (the sea) that ye mankind may seek of His bounty, and that happily ye may give thanks).[11]

" ربكم الذى يزجى لكم الفلك فى البحر لتبتغوا من فضله انه
كان بكم رحيما ـ و اذا مسكم الضر فى البحرضلّ من تدعون الّا
إياه ، فلما نجّكم الى البر أعرضتم و كان الأنسان كفورا "

(XVII:66—67)

(O mankind, your Lord is He Who driveth for you the ship upon the sea that ye may seek of His bounty. Lo! He was ever merciful toward you. And when harm toucheth you upon the sea, all unto whom ye cry for succour fail save Him alone, but when He bringeth you safe to land, ye turn away, for man was ever thankless.)[12]

"... او كظلمات فى بحر لجّىّ يغشاه موج من فوقه موج من فوقه سحاب ، ظلمات بعضها فوق بعض ... "

(XXIV:40)

(...Or as darkness on a vast, abysmal sea. There covereth him a wave, above which is a wave, above which is a cloud. Layer upon layer of darkness).[13]

Their Religious Thought

In spite of the fact that the pre-Islamic Arabs worshipped idols, they were idolaters only in a limited sense. In the depth of their hearts they believed not only in the oneness of Allah, but also in some of His attributes describing Him as Almighty, Creator, Compassionate, Forgiving and Rewarding, etc. They did not ascribe to their idols any divine powers. They were looked upon only as interecessors with Allah. They believed that the absolute authority to create, to benefit, to harm or to dispose of the affairs of the universe rested with Allah alone. Numerous instances can be quoted in support of this point from both the pre-Islamic Arabic poetry as well as the Qur'ãnic references to their religious thought. The following lines by the pre-Islamic poets clearly show different aspects of their perception of, and faith in, Allah.

Zuhayr:

"فلا تكتمن اللّه ما فى نفوسكم
ليخفى و مهما يكتم اللّه يعلم
يؤخر فيوضع فى كتاب فيدخر
ليوم الحساب او يعجل فينقم"[14]

(Do not conceal the secrets of your heart from Allah with a view to keeping them hidden, for whatever is concealed from Him, He is already aware of it.

You must be punished for your sin sooner or later. There is no escape from it. The punishment will befall you either soon in this very world, or in case of delay it will be recorded in a book for the Day of Judgement).[14]

Hãtim:

اما والذى لايعلم الغيب غيره
ويحيى العظام البيض وهى رميم[15]

(By Him none except Who knows the hidden and Who revives the white bones when they have rotted away).[15]

Ubayd bin al-Abras:

والله ليس له شريك
علام ماأخفت القلوب[16]

(Allah has taken unto Him no partner. He is fully aware of whatever is hidden in the hearts of people).[16]

من يسأل الناس يحرموه
وسائل الله لا يخيب[17]

(He who asks people for something, he is kept derprived of it, but if he asks Allah, he is not disappointed).[17]

Nãbighah al-Dhulyãnî:

الم تر ان الله أعطاك سورة
ترى كل ملك دونها يتذبذب[18]

(Do you not see that Allah has granted you a dignity, in the face of which every king keeps wavering).'[18]

Likewise, the picture of their religious thought as gleaned from the Qur'ãnic references to it further establishes that the pre-Islamic Arabs had faith in the unity of Allah as well as in His attributes of perfection long before the advent of Islam. The Qur'ãn has recorded their faith in Allah as their Creator in the following words:

"ولئن سألتهم من خلقهم ليقولن اللّٰه فأنّى يؤفكون ـ"

(XLIII:87)

(And if thou ask them who created them, they will surely say: Allah. How then are they turned away?)[19]

They also had faith in Allah as the Supreme Ruler Who disposed of all affairs of the universe according to His will. It was to Him alone that they turned for succour in the event of calamities. This is fully corroborated by the following verse:

"هو الذى يسيركم فى البر والبحر، حتى اذا كنتم فى الفلك
وجرين بهم بريح طيبة و فرحوا بها جاءتها ريح عاصف وّجاءهم
الموج من كل مكان وظنوا انهم احيط بهم دعوا اللّٰه مخلصين له الدين
لئن أنجيتنا من هذه لنكوننّ من الشاكرين ـ" (X:23)

(He it is Who maketh you to go on the land and the sea till, when ye are in the ships and they sail with them with a fair breeze and they are glad therein, a storm-wind reacheth them and the wave cometh unto them from every side and they deem that they are overwhelmed therein; then they cry unto Allah, making their faith pure for Him only; if Thou deliver us from this, we truly will be of the thankful).[20]

That they accorded merely an intermediary status to their idols is clearly mentioned in the following verses:

"ويعبدون من دون اللّٰه مالايضرهم ولا ينفعهمُ يقولون هؤلاء شفعاونا عنداللّٰه ـ " (X:19)

(They worship beside Allah that which neither hurteth them nor profiteth them, and they say: These are our intercessors with Allah):[21] Also

"والذين اتخذوا من دونه اولياء مانعبدهم الاّ ليقربونا الى اللّٰه زلفى ... " (XXXIX:3)

(And those who choose protecting friends beside Him say: We worship them only that they may bring us near unto Allah).[22]

It is interesting to note that the words Allah (the One God) and *Rabb* (Lord) are used in the Qur'ãn almost exactly in the same sense as perceived and used by the Arabs. The word Allah is used in the Qur'ãn about 2820 times, while the word *Rabb* is used 976 times.[23]

The above verses clearly show that the Arabs did not believe in polytheism in a real sense of the term. They neither associated equally competent and independent gods with Allah, nor did they recognize any eternal entity for their idols. As such they cannot be put on a par with the other polytheistic nations like the Indians, the Romans and the Zoroastrians, etc.

Besides, there existed in Arabia a group of monotheists, who felt disgust at idol-worship and forsook it. They longed for the religion of Abraham and tried to find out what had been its teaching. Such seekers of the truth were known as *Hunafã*' (the upright). They held Allah to be perfect from all points of view, Who has taken neither wife nor son nor partner. Of them mention may be made of the following:

Zayd bin 'Umar bin Nafîl; Arbab bin Riãb; Suwayd bin 'Ãmir al-Mustalaqî; As'ad Abû Karb al-Hamîrî; Kab' bin Salma bin Zuhayr; Abû Qays Sarha bin Abî Anas; 'Abd al-Tãnija bin Tha'lab bin Wabra; 'Allãf bin Shihãb al-Tamîmî; Umayya ibn Abî al-Salt; and Waraqa ibn Nawfal, etc. The noblest of them Prophet Muhammad also belonged to this group."[24]

As regards the source of their religious throught, it should be remembered that they had inherited their monotheistic religious ideas from their ancestors by virtue of being the descendants of the prophets Abraham and Ismael. It was Abraham who had built in Makkah the Grand Mosque, the Ka'ba, for the worship of Allah. Moreover, Islam never claimed to preach a new religion. It only revived the religion of Abraham and gave it a final shape through Prophet Muhammad. The Qur'ãn has referred to this fact in the following verses:

"وقالوا كونوا هودا او نصارى تهتدوا ، قل بل ملة ابراهيم حنيفا ،
و ماكان من المشركين -" (II:135)

(And they say: Be Jews or Christians, then ye will be rightly guided. Say unto them, O Muhammad: Nay, but we follow the religion of Abraham, the upright, and he was not of the idolaters).[25]

"ثم اوحينا إليك ان اتبع ملة ابراهيم حنيفا ، وما كان من
المشركين " - (XVI:123)

(And afterward We inspired thee, O Muhammad:

Follow the religion of Abraham, as one by nature upright. He was not of the idolaters).[26]

"ومن أحسن دينا ممن أسلم وجهه للّه وهو محسن واتبع ملّة ابراهيم حنيفا واتخذ اللّه ابراهيم خليلا ـ" (IV:125)

(Who is better in religion than he who surrendered his purpose to Allah while doing good to men and followeth the tradition of Abraham, the upright? Allah Himself chose Abraham for friend).[27]

Linguistic Evidence of their Intellectual Awakening

The very language of the Arabs reveals that they were a wise, eloquent and scientific people. They had a very rich language. It was in its perfect and highly finished form long before the advent of Islam. No other language seems capable of exercising over the minds of its users such irresistible influence as Arabic. They were rightly proud of their eloquent tongue which was quite capable of scientific expression. As described by the renowned Arab scholar al-Jãhiz, "Wisdom has alighted on three things: the brain of the Franks, the hands of the Chinese and the tongue of the Arabs."[28]

Arabic language is based on durable, firm and flexible structures that have enabled it to live for over fifteen centuries in its classical form, not only as language of the religion of Islam but also as language of the Arab mass media. No other language can compare with it in this respect. Its unique quality to retain its basic structure and vitality is described by a modern Western philologist Jaroslav Stetkevych in the following words:

"It has lived for one million and a half essentially unchanged, usually gaining, never completely losing. Venus-like, it was born in a perfect state

> of beauty, and it has preserved that beauty in spite of all the hazards of history and all the corrosive forces of time... It has known austerity, holy ecstasy and voluptuousness, bloom and decadence. It exuberated in times of splendour and persisted through times of adversity in a state of near-hybernation. But when it awoke again, it was the same language."[29]

Arabic is a most logically developed language. It is still one of the unsolved mysteries of philology as to how this language, as developed and perfected by the pre-Islamic Arabs, could acquire the capacity of adapting itself to the needs of a highly urbanized and articulate culture without getting distorted. The French Orientalist Ernest Renan, who is otherwise known to be a biased critic of Arab legacy and culture, has expressed this mystery as follows:

> "One of the strangest events in human history and whose mystery is difficult to unravel, is the spread of the Arabic language. This language was unknown at the beginning, then all of a sudden it reached the height of excellence..., and there has occured no important change in it until now. It has no childhood and no old age. It appeared for the first time complete and consolidated....One of the amazing things about this national language is that it was born and reached the degree of existence in the midst of deserts and in a nomadic nation, and excelled its sister languages in vocabulary, precision of meanings, and beauty of its structure."[30]

The literary heritage left by the pre-Islamic Arabs also throws sufficient light on the vividness of their imagination, power of expression and minute observation. The elaborate form and technical perfection of their poems and odes fully establish that they are works of highly finished art. They are regarded by Arab linguists as models of unapproachable excellence. Sir Charles Lyall has commented on the form and matter of these highly developed productions in the following words:

> "The number and complexity of the measures which they use, their established laws of quantity and rhyme, and the uniform manner in which they introduce the subject of their poems, notwithstanding the distance which often separated one composer from another, all point to a long previous study and cultivation of the art of expression and capacities of their language,—a study of which no record now remains."[31]

Prof. H.A.R. Gibb, has expressed his appreciation of the pre-Islamic poems in the following words:

> "At one moment Arabia seems in a literary sense empty and dumb except for some votive and businesslike inscriptions in a variety of dialects. At the next, companies of poets spring up all over Northern Arabia, reciting complex odes, qasidas, in which a series of themes are elaborated with unsurpassed vigour, vividness of imagination, and precision of imagery, in an infinitely rich and highly articulated language, showing no traces of dialect and cast into complex and flexible metrical rhyme throughout the poem."[32]

From what has been discussed above it is quite clear that the pre-Islamic Arabs were an eloquent, energetic, brave and scientific people with tremendous capacity for observation, assimilation and acclimatization as well as making sacrifices for the sake of the ideals cherished by them. They had been inheritors of the religion of Abraham with the difference that in the course of time it had become distorted with the addition of superstitions, idol-worship and folklore. What harmed them most was their haughtiness, intertribal rivalry and war-like spirit rather than their ignorance and stupidity. In short, they had all the ingredients of a powerful nation which needed to be tamed, sharpened and channelized by a civilizing force. That was the main reason why it did not take them much time to emerge as a cultured and strong nation under the banner of Islam. As is well-known, within a century after their rise they not only became the masters of a big empire, an empire greater than that of Rome at its zenith, but also contributed a great deal to the cause of knowledge and learning.

Finally, I thank you one again for the patient hearing you have so kindly given to me.

NOTES AND REFERENCES

1. *Diwãn-ul-Hamãsah*, compiled by Mohd. I'zãz 'Alî. Deoband, p. 115.
2. The Qur'ãn: XVII—31.
3. الدكتور رشاد محمد خليل": تكوين الفكر العربي قبل الاسلام" في مجلة "اللسان العربي" المجلد الرابع عشر، الجزء الأول، ص ٩٥
4. *Tãrîkh Ibn Khaldû*, Vol. II, pp. 167-168, quoted by Dr. Rashãd.
5. Muhammad 'Abdûh: *Risãlat-ul-Tawhîd*, p. 180, quoted by Dr. Rashãd, op.cit., p. 95.
6. Dr. Rashãd, op.cit., p. 96.
7. الدكتور رياض محمود: "العرب و الملاحة" في محلة "العربي" الكويت، اكتوبر، ١٩٧١، ص ٣٦ –
8. The Seven Poems suspended in the Temple at Makkah tr. by Capt. F.E. Johnson, pp. 32-33.
9. *The M'uallaqah* by 'Amr bin Kulthûm.
10. M.M. Pickthall: "The Meaning of the Glorious Koran", p. 382.
11. *Ibid.*, p. 196.
12. *Ibid.*, p. 208.
13. *Ibid.,* p. 256.
14. *The Mu'allaqah* by Zuhayr.
15. *Dîwan Hãtim*, quoted by Dr. Rahsãd.
16. *The Mu'allaqah* by 'Ubaid bin al-Arabs, quoted by Dr. Rashãd.
17. *Mukhtar*, quoted by Dr. Rashãd, p. 98.

18. *Ibid.,* p. 102.
19. M.M. Pickthall, op.cit., p. 352.
20. *Ibid.*, p. 159.
21. *Ibid.,* p. 158.
22. *Ibid.*, p. 329.
23. Dr. Rashãd in "*al-Lisãn-ul-Arabĩ*", Vol. XVIII, Part I, p. 120.
24. *Ibid.,* p. 119.
25. M.M. Pickthall, op.cit., p. 45.
26. *Ibid.*, p. 203.
27. *Ibid.*, p. 91.
28. P.K. Hitti: *History of the Arabs*, p. 90-91.
29. Prof. M.A. Saleem Khan: "Arabs, Arabic and the Future" in *al-Lisan-ul-'Arabi*, Vol. XVII, Part I, p. XXIX.
30 *Ibid.*
31. R.A. Nicholson: *Literary History of the Arabs*, pp. 75-76.
32. Prof. M.A. Saleem Khan, op.cit., p. XXIX.

PRESIDENTIAL ADDRESS: ISLAMIC STUDIES SECTION,
33rd Session, A.I.O.C., Calcutta (1986)

Fellow Delegates and Friends,

I am grateful beyond words to the authorities of the All-India Oriental Conference for the great honour they have done me by electing me to preside over the Islamic Studies Section of the 33rd Session of the Conference that is being held at Calcutta under the auspices of the Asiatic Society. I deem it a rare privilege to get an opportunity to address such a distinguished gathering of learned scholars who have assembled here from all over the country. I am aware of my limitations, yet I am confident that with your co-operation I shall be able to conduct the business of this section to the satisfaction of all concerned.

It is customary with Sectional Presidents on such occasions to give an account of the work done in their respective fields during the interval between the past and present sessions. But I crave your indulgence for my deviation from this practice and seek your permission to touch upon a theme of general interest which concerns us most at present, namely, attitude of the West towards Islam and Muslim civilization. This will be followed by a discussion on the need to highlight the contribution of Islam to the advancement of science and civilization.

It is sad to note that Islam which contributed a great deal to human thought and progress during the early years of its history, remains a misunderstood and misrepresented religion not only by non-Muslims, but also by such Muslims themselves who consider all kinds of original and creative thinking in the context of the modern socio-economic and political developments as unpardonable acts of blasphemy.

It is generally contended by non-Muslim writers on Islam that lasting peace and co-operation between Muslims and non-Muslims is not possible as the former are under religious obligation to carry on the *jihad* (the holy war) against the latter for the purpose of compelling them to accept the Muslim faith. Besides, judging from the deplorable political and economic as well as moral and intellectual decay of the present-day Muslims, they tend to consider it as outmoded and antagonistic to scientific development. They also look upon it as a şymbol of backwardness and primitive barbarism.

Furthermore, being ignorant of the moral, spiritual and humanistic values of Islam, they deride its teachings and belittle its importance as a civilizing factor. While seeking to support their viewpoints, they hold that the system which approves of slavery, degrades the position of women in society and encourages polygamy, provides for the holy war for the purpose of proselytization, prescribes such punishments as stoning to death, mutilation, whipping, etc., is not only obsolete and antiquated, but also contrary to all forms of human behaviour.

It is worthy of mention in this context that the mistrust about Islam is not the result of independent thinking of the Western people, but rather it is closely related with their age-old hostile attitude towards this religion and its followers. This hostility generated mainly by the triumph of Islam over Judaism and Christianity in the Middle Ages, seems to have been a powerful factor in determining the Western attitude towards it. As is well-known, the successors of Prophet Muhammad conquered Christianity in Yemen, Syria, Egypt and Constantinople. The fight continued for several centuries between Christendom and Islam. The war was not limited to swords and weapons alone. It spread out to the fields of debate and controversy also. This gave birth to a large number of Orientalists who produced a vast body of literature on Islam which is replete with grave and mischievous inaccuracies. Since Islam still remains the most formidable and potential rival to the modern West, their hostility is reflected in a countless ways even now.[1]

By and large until the mid-eighteenth century, Orientalists were Biblical scholars, who wrote with the missionary zeal to distort the image of Islam by their unfair criticism of the Islamic way of life. They painted Prophet Muhammad in the blackest of colours, and ridiculed his teachings. They described Muslims as savage conquerors who carried fire and swords wherever they went. They also charged them with having destroyed palaces, churches, temples and libraries. They mixed up historical facts with fiction and presented them as truth. In this way they invented and perpetuated false notions about Islam and Muslims in an organised way, and produced a large number of books in condemnation of Islamic tenets. It is estimated that around 60,000 books dealing with the Near Orient were written by Orientalists between 1800 and 1950, while the number of Oriental books produced in the East about the West is quite negligible.[2]

If we go through the works of the Orientalists, it appears that, barring a few exceptions, like Godfrey Higgins, Thomas Carlyle, John Devenport, Lamartine, etc., majority of them wrote on Islam with the sole objective of refuting the concept of the divine origin of this religion as well as representing Prophet Muhammad as a 'scheming impostor', 'a falsehood incarnate'. They looked upon Islam as a symbol of barbarism and a religion of sensuality. They supported this point by telling that the Prophet permitted poligamy, and he himself had a great many wives to satisfy his sensual lust. "What an idea of Islam! But it is the idea in the minds of ninety-nine out of one hundred Britishers".[3]

The critics further argued that the Prophet, far from being divinely inspired, was predominantly dependent upon Jewish and Christian sources in the formulation of his doctrines. For example, C.C. Torrey in his book *The Jewish Foundation of Islam* asserted that the Prophet was a disciple of the synagogue, while W. Ahrens maintained that the Christian influences were decisive for him.[4] They further held that Islam, by its immutable dogmas, paralysed the brain and killed all initiative. Consider the following statement given by Andre Servier in support of this point in his book *Islam and the Psychology of the Musulman:*

> "How is it that the Syrians, the Egyptians, the Berbers, as soon as they became Islamised, lost the energy, the intelligence and the spirit of initiative they exhibited under the domination of Greece and Rome? How has it come about that the Arabs themselves, who, according to the historians, were the professors of science and philosophy in the West, can have forgotten all their brilliant accomplishments and have sunk into a state of ignorance that today relegates them to the barbarous nations?"[5]

In order to be acquainted with the true nature of Orientalism, a passing reference to a few eminent Orientalists would not be out of place here. In his *Weltgeschichte* (1881-1888), Ranke sought to expose the inferiority of Islam by speaking of it as defeated by the Germanic-Romanic peoples; and in his *Historiche Fragments*, Burckhardt condemned it as wretched and trivial, while Noldeke declared in 1887 that his main objective as an Orientalist had been to confirm his "low opinion" of the Eastern peoples.[6]

Similarly, Ignaz Goldziher, though he appreciated the tolerance of Islam towards other religions, bitterly criticised what he called Muhammad's anthropomorphism; Duncan Black Macdonald considered Islam as heretical Christianity; Carl Becker looked upon Islamic civilization as a sadly undeveloped one; C. Snouck Hurgronji's studies of Islamic mysticism made him critical of its limitations; while Louis Massignon remained critical of Islam for its rejection of the idea of incarnation. As described by Edward W. Said, the above five scholars were the architects of the image of Islam in the West in the late nineteenth and early twentieth century.[7]

The twentieth century Orientalists fared no better than their predecessors. They never tired of subjecting the tenets of Islam to biased criticism. They attributed the overall backwardness of the present-day Muslims to what they regarded as the element of anti-humanism in Islamic civilization by depicting Islam as the enemy of scientific thought and progress. For instance, Wollaston in 1905, Lammens in 1926, Anderson and Watt in the 1960s only reiterated the baseless assumption that the Qur'ãn was the result of wishful thinking and that "it could have been written by any Arab who is acquainted with the general outline of the Jewish history and of the traditions of his own country and possessed some poetic fire and fancy."[8]

Besides, even better informed 'enlightened' Western historians are not only found sunk in depths of ignorance in regard to the dynamism and humanistic aspects of Islam, but also have consistently and systematically played down its contribution to human thought and progress. While recording the story of civilization, they usually jump from the Greeks to the Renaissance as though the intermediary period of the Middle Ages was totally barren from the point of view of the development of science. Bernal's book: *Science in History*, in four volumes of 1325 pages, is an example of this pattern, in which the author has devoted only 10 pages to Islamic science.[9]

Again, C.E.M. Joad, author of *the Story of Civilization*, while talking of the contribution of religion to the advancement of human civilization, did not include Prophet Muhammad among the great religious teachers chosen by him. Emphasizing the civilizing importance of the religious teachings of Buddha, Lao-Tse, Confucius and Jesus Christ, he says: "If man lived the kind of life which these four great religious teachers urged them to live, the world would be much better and happier, and at the same time a more civilized place than it is or ever has been".[10] It is indeed surprising that the author has not given even a passing reference to the great role played by Prophet Muhammad and his followers in advancing the cause of knowledge and learning. On the contrary, he has dismissed the Arab caliphs and rulers as uncivilized. Interestingly enough, his source of information about them was confined to the Arabian Nights. To quote his own words:

> "But in the main the princes and the princesses, the caliphs whom you meet in the Arabian Nights, and the rich and powerful of all countries, were content, as most people have always been content to get what they liked and to enjoy it. At bottom most of these kings and rulers were just treacle toffee eaters. So the Empires and the caliphs and the kings and princes don't for the most part come into this book."[11]

Similarly, the biased Orientalists never tired of charging Islam with being militant and intolerant towards members of other religions. They held the view that the savage nomadic Arab tribes spread the Islamic religion by the sword and flame between the seventh and ninth centuries. Dr. S. Margoliouth has highlighted this charge in the following words:

> "Towards the end of the Prophet's career an injunction is given quite in accordance with Noah's

> prayer: When the sacred months are ended, slay the associators wheresoever ye find them. When ye meet those that disbelieve, behead them, until ye have made a massacre of them, and then make fast their bonds; after which be gracious or take ransom.... In accordance with this order the Islamic system recognised two communities as having the right to exist: the Muslims, who were to be dominant, and the People of the Book, who were to be subjugated: all others were to be exterminated."[12]

From what precedes, it is sufficiently clear that Islam is fundamentally misrepresented in the West, and through it all over the world. The above-mentioned Edward W. Said, a Palestinian scholar, has in his book *Orientalism* very successfully exposed the fallacies of the Orientalists. It is undoubtedly a scholarly work in which he has given a brilliant and far-reaching cirtique of the attitudes that the West has traditionally assumed towards the East. He is perfectly right when he says that Western anti-Semitism and Orientalism resemble each other very closely. He further denounced such Orientalists by saying that "They are nor academics, but beneficiaries of the academic study of the Orient."[13]

Here I would like to emphasize that the Oriental scholars of Islamic studies cannot escape the responsibility of correcting the distortions made by the Orientalists. A few words regarding rebuttal of some of their main charges may not be out of place in this context. Contrary to their accusations, Islam remains a scientific way of living which aims at both spiritual uplift and material well-being of man. It came to give him confidence in his destiny by enlightening him both in relation to his Creator and the created world. He is described as master of the universe and the noblest creature. Everything else in the universe is created to serve him.

Even the angels are below him in rank and dignity. He is ordained to perform his role as benefactor of humanity by establishing and promoting on earth a highly civilized society based on the ethical framework of Islam for peaceful co-existence comprising tolerance, freedom of faith and conscience, universal brotherhood of mankind as well as principles of humanism.

Far from setting unattainable ideals for its followers, Islam is a practical and utilitarian religion in the sense that all its teachings of ethics and virtues, individual and public morality, its inspiration for cultivation of knowledge and learning, its political structure as well as its purely religious duties centering on the five pillars of Islam i.e., the profession of faith, prayers, fasting, alms-giving and pilgrimage-they are all designed to promote human happiness and prosperity. It also gave a very comprehensive concept of worship which consists not only in prayers of its followers, but also in his active participation in exploring and pressing into the service of man all the seen and unseen forces and objects of Nature for the welfare of humanity at large. As such all the actions and functions, efforts and endeavours made by man in this direction right from going to bed for rest and sleep to sacrificing his life in the cause of justice and truth, are regarded as worship in Islam. No wonder, a true follower of Islam is simultaneously a benefactor of humanity as well as worshipper of Allah.

Secular and tolerant political spirit of Islam is another great contribution of this religion to the advancement of human civilization. It is common knowledge that lack of tolerance and courtesy on the part of one religious community towards another often triggers off communal disturbances that threaten the very stability of society. But Islam has struck at the very root of this problem by making it binding upon its followers to develop a tolerant and secular attitude towards members of other religions. One chief feature of Islamic tolerance is that it constitutes an essential part of this religion, as it is strictly enjoined in a number of Qur'ãnic verses and Traditions of Prophet Muhammad. They not only prohibit Muslims from imposing their faith on non-Muslims, but also exhort them to treat the latter gently and justly. They are also enjoined to practice utmost restraint, endurance and patience in their treatment of non-Muslims as well as to respect their prophets and religious authorities.

It is worthy of mention in this context that Prophet Muhammad himself meted out a very kind and generous treatment to non-Muslims not only in the early years of his prophethood, but also in the later years when he was at the height of his power and at the head of a large army. Numerous instances can be quoted in support of this point. Here it will suffice to mention that the way he treated the delegation of the Christians of Najran has no parallel in the history of other conquerors. He not only played host to them and lodged them in the Prophetic Mosque, but also permitted them to offer prayers on Christian lines in the same Mosque. Perhaps, a similar example of secularism is hard to find elsewhere.[14]

Likewise, the Orientalists' charge regarding poligamy which is described by them as one of the chief offences of Islam against the fair sex is based on their ignorance of the spirit behind the Islamic sanction in this regard. It is true that Islam did not reject poligamy outright, but at the same time it never encouraged it, nor did it make it binding upon its followers. It is generally missed by the critics that the humanised from of poligamy as retained by Islam is more of a social responsibility on the part of the poligamous Muslim male than of a means to enjoy the luxury of plurality of wives. The example of Prophet Muhammad himself is a sufficient proof in support of this point. Till the age of fifty-two he had only one wife named Bibi Khadijah, who was fifteen years senior to him. After her death he contracted a number of marriages. Except for Bibi Aishah all his wives were widows. He married them with a view to providing them with a home and a position they could not otherwise enjoy. For instance, Bibi Salma had a number of children when her husband died in the battle of Uhud. It was only out of sympathy for her as well as in recognition of the sacrifices made by her husband that the Prophet married her. His remaining marriages were also motivated by similar considerations. This shows that by being poligamous he was not satisfying his lust but acting as a reformer.

Similarly, the Islamic concept of universal brotherhood of mankind is the pressing need of the hour. This is one of the essentials of a civilized society. As is well-known, false notion of racial superiority has been a major hurdle in achieving this goal. It has already caused a great deal of bloodshed among different human races. But Islam demolished the age-old barriers of caste and colour by asserting common origin of all human beings. Xenophobia, racism and apartheid, the main ills of the modern superiority-conscious Western materialistic civilization, are just alien to Islam, as it recognises piety as the sole basis of nobility and superiority. Undoubtedly, this concept develops in man an optimistic attitude towards life by inspiring him to attain superiority through noble deeds.

There is also the provision of *Ijtihad* (original thinking) in Islam for framing fresh laws to satisfy new conditions in accordance with the spirit of Islam. This keeps the evolutionary spirit of Muslim jurisprudence alive as well as authorises its followers to legislate for themselves to meet their modern requirements. Its doors are as wide open today as they might have been in the times of Prophet Muhammad and his immediate successors.

These secular and humanistic aspects of Islam are some of the important ingredients of Islamic civilization which need to be introduced in their proper persepectives to the modern scientific world confronted with a number of challenges that have not only aggravated human miseries, but also threaten the very stability of society.

Now I shall proceed to make a few more suggestions for our general guidance. First, the part played by the Muslims in advancing the cause of knowledge and learning, especially in the fields of natural and exact sciences, needs to be properly and adequately highlighted, because it was their contributions in these fields of knowledge that form the connecting link between the Greco-Roman classical age and the modern scientific era.

Two important characteristics of the Muslims' ethics of science are worthy of mention here. First, instead of keeping their knowledge of science secret, they disseminated it by providing educational facilities on a large scale. It was their transmission of knowledge to the West that quickened the process of Renaissance and put Europe on its way to the modern scientific age. Secondly, in contrast to the Western vision of science, the Muslims cultivated it only for constructive purposes. The famous Muslim scientist al-Razi categorically refused to prepare deadly drugs that could harm human beings. Had this example been followed by modern scientists, humanity would have been saved from the clutches of science-based harmful inventions. But it is a matter of great pity that the works of Muslim scientists in various fields have not yet been sufficiently studied and acknowledged. It is now high time that scholars pursuing Islamic studies should undertake, without further loss of time, a systematic and comprehensive study of their contributions to the advancement of science, so that their role as bearers of the torch of culture and civilization may be properly assessed and appreciated.

Publication of unpublished texts and manuscripts is another important work which remains to be done on an urgent basis. Of the large numbers of manuscripts on different subjects of Islamic studies that are lying scattered in different parts of the world, there are thousands of valuable manuscripts in the libraries of India also, especially, the Govt. Raza Library, Rampur, the Khuda Bukhsh Library, Patna, the State Public Library, Hyderabad, the Arabic and Persian Research Institute, Tonk, the Asiatic Society Library, Calcutta, and the Central Public Library, Bhopal. While undertaking this job, it is desirable that priority should be given to the works on scientific subjects. Again, our search for scientific works should not be confined to those in Arabic alone, but in all the Oriental languages used by the Muslims, especially Persian and Turkish, as a great deal of source material on these subjects is to be found in these languages also.

It is a matter of utmost satisfaction that interest in Islamic studies has considerably increased in modern times all over the world. A number of universities and institutes in our own country provide facilities for study and research in this discipline. It is studied as a separate subject in the universities of Aligarh, Delhi, Kashmir, Calcutta, Hyderabad and Kerala. Some academic journals of international repute devoted to Islamic research and scholarship are also being published here. For example, the quarterly journals *Islam and the Modern Age* and *Islamic Culture* are published by the Zakir Hussain Institute of Islamic Studies, New Delhi, and the Islamic Culture Board, Hyderabad, respectively.

The Indian Institute of Islamic Studies established by the learned and generous philanthropist Hakim Abdul Hameed at Tughlaqabad, New Delhi, deserves special mention. It is doing commendable work under the able guidance of its director Syed Ausaf Ali. It provides adequate infrastructural facilities to scholars for study and research. Its library is stocked with up-to-date publications. It is equipped with a complete Microfilm Unit with Mobile teams, a Preservation, Restoration and Binding Division and a Documentation Centre called the Islamic Information Bureau. Efforts are also being made to acquire important manuscripts or their microfilms. It has already collected over 5,000 rare manuscripts on different branches of Islamic learning. It is on the mailing list of about 38 journals in Arabic, 34 in Urdu, 4 in Persian and 13 journals in English. It also publishes three learned periodicals in English, namely, *Studies in Islam, Islamic and Comparative Law Quarterly* and *Bulletin of Comparative Religion.*

While it is highly desirable that some more centres of Islamic studies should be established in other parts of the country, it is equally important that the existing ones should be refurbished and revitalized by making them well-equipped to meet the needs of researchers. It is difficult to understand why a department of Islamic studies could not be started in any of the numerous universities of Madhya Pradesh. Bhopal University is very suitably located for this purpose. Establishment of a full-fledged department of Islamic studies at this university is not only a long felt academic need, but also it will make its existing School of Comparative Languages and Culture more purposeful. It is gratifying to note that a centre of study and research on Islamic culture and civilization was recently started at this prestigious Asiatic Society. Since this is the oldest Asiatic Society founded as long back as 1784 as well as an institution of national importance, it is hoped that this Institute will soon develop into a big centre of Islamic studies.

Lastly, I shall be failing in my duty if I do not take into consideration the traditions of Islamic learning being carried on in our traditional institutions and seminaries. They not only train and teach students in the traditional Islamic sciences such as Tafsir, Hadith, Fiqh, al-Kalam, Theology and early Islamic History, but also publish books and periodicals on them. They continue to hold religious leadership of the Muslim masses; and their verdicts on controversial religious issues are by and large considered final. In spite of the fact that the old classical methods of teaching and study on the pattern of *Dars-e-Nizami* are still adhered to in these institutions, yet some of them have shown good results. Of them mention may be made of Dar-ul-Muṣannifin, Azamgarh; Nadwat-ul-Ulama Lucknow; Dar-ul-'Ulûm, Deoband; Mazahir-ul-'Ulûm, Saharanpur; Jaṃi'ah Salafiyah, Varanasi; Jami'ah Nizamiyah, Hyderabad, and others. But unfortunately, there exists a wide gap between the scholars of these traditional institutions and those of our modern institutes and universities. It is desirable that some sort of co-ordination and co-operation should be brought about between both groups of scholars. This will not only bridge the existing gap, but also enable them to carry on their work more efficiently.

Finally, I thank you once again for the honour and trust you have given to me and patient hearing you have so kindly accorded to me.

NOTES AND REFERENCES

1. Maryam Jameelah, *Islam Versus Ahl Al-Kitab*, p. xviii.
2. Edward W. Said, *Orientalism*, London, 1978, p. 204.
3. Lord Headly, *A Western Awakening to Islam*, p. 11.
4. *Studies on Islam*, edited by Marlin L. Swartz, Oxford University Press, 1981, p. 87.
5. Andre Servier, *Islam and the Psychology of the Musulman* (English translation), pp. 2-5.
6. Edward W. Said, *op.cit.*, pp. 208-209.
7. *Ibid.*, p. 209.
8. Mohammad Khalifa, *The Sublime Qur'ãn and Orientalism*, 1983, pp. 10-11.
9. Mahmoud Dhaudi: "Contemporary Civilization's Crisis and Islamic Ethical Principles of Science" in *Islam Today*, No. 1. Morocco, p. 37.
10. C.E.M. Joad, *The Story of Civilization*, London, 1946, p. 29.
11. *Ibid.*, p. 15.
12. Dr. S. Margoliouth, *Mohammad*, p. 86-87.
13. Edward W. Said, *op.cit.*, p. 223.
14. See "Tolerance in Islam" by Abdul Ali, in *Islamic Culture* (April, 1982), Hyderabad, pp. 105-120.

PRESIDENTIAL ADDRESS: ISLAMIC STUDIES SECTION,

35th Session, A.I.O.C., Hardwar (1990)

Fellow Delegates and Friends,

I am deeply grateful to the authorities of the All-India Oriental Conference for considering me worthy of the honour they have conferred upon me by electing me as president of the Islamic Studies Section of the 35th Session of the Conference that is being held at Hardwar, under the auspices of the Gurukul Kangri Vishwavidyalaya, a great centre of Oriental Studies. While accepting the heavy responsibility of this high office, I am fully conscious of my limitations. Yet I trust that with your help and co-operation I shall be able to perform the duties assigned to me.

At the outset I want to make it clear that instead of indulging in generalities and monotonous repetition of problems, difficulties and suggestions, I propose to take up in my address the treatment of a particular topic relating to a neglected area of research which I hope would be more useful and informative to the Orientalists in general and to the scholars of Islamic Studies in particular who are engaged in serious research on Islamic thought and heritage. That is that the hitherto little-studied but important aspects of the part played by the Muslims as harbingers of the modern scientific era need to be carefully analyzed, critically appreciated and introduced to the academic world. It is sad to note that adequate systematic attention has not yet been paid to the study and evaluation of the scientific contributions of the medieval Muslims, although much impressive work has been done on various other aspects of their legacy. Hundreds of books have been written by both Muslim and non-Muslim authors on different historical, political, literary and theological facets of Islamic heritage with all sorts of hair-splitting on them which in some cases proved futile and caused deviation from the dynamic spirit of Islam. Even their philosophical contributions have also been dealt with adequately to a certain extent. Needless to say that the current backwardness of the Muslims in general in the world of science together with their division into different warring sects is the result of such deviation caused and hastened, among other factors, by unimaginative, clerical and sectarian writings produced negligently of the Qur'ãnic mission of *tawhîd* and welfare to humanity at large. As a consequence of this development, the pivotal point of the Qur'ãnic wisdom embodied in the following and like verses became the first casualty:

> Whoever does an atom of good, he shall see the result of it, and whoever does an atom of evil, he shall see the consequence of it.[1]
>
> He gives wisdom unto whom He wills, and whosoever is given wisdom, he is indeed given lot of good.[2]
>
> Allah will exalt those who believe among you, and those who have knowledge, to high ranks. Allah is aware of what you do.[3]
>
> O those who believe! Stand firmly on the side of justice, as witnesses to Allah even if it be against yourselves, or your parents, or your kin....[4]

The above-mentioned deviation from the spirit of Islam gave birth to numerous other ills that retarded the growth of creative thought among the Muslims. They now became lethargic and dogmatic instead of remaining dynamic and scientific. They also ceased to be inspired by the original sources of Islam, i.e., the Qur'ãn and the *Sunnah.* This gave rise to the doctrine of *taqlîd* (conservative conformity), the followers of which made the Muslim jurisprudence static by maintaining that it was binding upon the believers to follow the rulings of the great jurists of the past, keeping thereby the doors of *ijtihãd* (fresh speculation) closed to the Muslims. But that was a sad development in the history of Islam as it was contrary to its inner impulse. It only denotes the lethargy that had overtaken the decadent Muslim world.

It is worthy of mention in this context that the scientific and intellectual foundations of Islam, as repeatedly emphasized in the Qur'ãn, have not yet been given their due importance. While the Qur'ãnic exhortations for the study and investigation of natural phenomena were taken very seriously by the early Muslims, they were unfortunately neglected by their later brethren. The Qur'ãn which is believed by the Muslims as the last revealed Book deserves to be studied more objectively. The modern scientific discoveries in different branches of knowledge can serve as an aid to a better appreciation of its miraculous nature.

Obviously, this assertion is made on the basis of the fact that there is nothing in the Qur'ãn which does not appeal to reason and intellect. It has ordained various measures to enable man to promote his critical acumen and intellectual capacity for a better perception of the surroundings around him. First, it seeks to purge the human mind of all sorts of conjecture, illusion and empty guesswork. Secondly, man is repeatedly asked in the Qur'ãn to assert his reason and intellect to acquire knowledge. Thirdly, it exhorts him to observe and investigate natural phenomena with a view to getting acquainted with the Laws of Nature. According to the renowned scientist Professor Muhammad Abdus Salam, seven hundred and fifty verses of the Qur'ãn (almost one-eighth of the Book) emphasise reflection on the Laws of Nature, with examples drawn from cosmology, physics, biology and medicine.[5] There is not even a single verse in the Qur'ãn dealing with natural phenomena which contradics what is known for certain from the discoveries in modern sciences.[6] This fact is acknowledged by Maurice Bucaille in the introductory chapter of his book *The Bible, the Qur'ãn and Science* in the following words:

> "The Qur'ãn did not contain a single statement that was assailable from a modern scientific point of view."

By doing so the Qur'ãn has not only stirred man's intellectual curiosity, but also advanced his scientific knowledge about the universe. There are a number of passages in it that took man to the utmost heights of human knowledge by disclosing some secrets of Nature which modern sciences have taken hundreds of years to verify and establish. For example, fertilization of trees by winds has only recently been discovered by science, to which the Qur'ãn has referred in the following words:

> "And We send the winds fertilizing."[7]

Again, now it is fully established by science that everything exists in pairs as male and female including the rock crystals and electricity.[8] Consider the following verse in this connection:

> "Praise be to Him Who created all things in pairs, of that which the earth grows, and of their own kind, and of kinds which they know not."[9]

Likewise, the Qur'ãn teaches man pure science when it alludes to rotation of the earth and other celestial bodies in clear terms as follows:

> "And He it is Who created the night and the day, and the sun and the moon. They float, each in an orbit."[10]

Inspired by these and like Qur'ãnic verses together with numerous Apostolic Traditions, the Muslims, both Arab and non-Arab, were filled with the spirit of scientific enquiry, developed a keen sense of intellectual curiosity and contributed a great deal to the development of human thought and progress. But it is a matter of deep regreat that there remains in our educational institutions a definite lack of systematic study of the intellectual heritage of the Muslims. It is only at the cost of historical justice that the fertile period of nearly one thousand years of Muslim intellectual ascendancy during the Middle Ages is almost totally neglected even by modern writers in their historical accounts of science and civilization. They tend to jump from the Greeks to the Renaissance without making proper acknowledgement of the contributions made by the Muslims to the development of philosophy, natural sciences, medicine, mathematics, astronomy, etc. Thus the Islamic intellectual heritage remains one of the neglected areas of research in Islamic Studies which deserves the attention of devoted specialists on this subject. A brief introduction to their achievements in some of these fields is attempted below as specimens of their scientific heritage, on account of which they deserve to be honoured as the main connecting link between the Greco-Roman classical age and modern civilization.

Medicine:

The science of medicine developed a great deal at the hands of the Arabs and Muslims who cultivated it with great zeal and made spectacular achievements in almost all the branches connected with the curative science, namely, clinical treatment, pharmacy, surgery, the art of nursing patients in hospitals, ophthalmology, anatomy, psychotherapy, etc. It is they who introduced experimental methods into the study of diseases and their treatment at a time when their European counterparts looked upon some serious diseases like small-pox and epidemics as manifestations of the wrath of and punishment from God.

It should be clearly borne in mind in this context that the history of the Muslim legacy to medicine begins right from the lifetime of Prophet Muhammad (peace be upon him) himself, whose teachings brought about a revolution in the art of preserving and restoring health by laying down fundamental principles as preventive measures for the improvement of both physical and psychic hygiene.[11]

It goes to the credit of the Muslims that they started practical education for medical students in their hospitals. They were the first to require their physicians and druggists to submit to a test before they could be permitted to practice their profession. They also established asylums for the care and treatment of the insane while such patients in the West were kept confined in chains and severely beaten.

The Muslim hospital system was organised on modern lines. There were different wards for different diseases. Each ward had a number of specialized physicians. Both physicians and paramedical personnel, like attendants, technicians and druggists worked on shift basis, who were available in their respective wards and rooms during their duty hours. Each hospital had laboratories, dispensaries, outdoor clinics, kitchens and baths. It was equipped with a library also. The Ibn Tûlûn Hospital of Egypt is said to have contained more than one hundred thousand books on different subjects.

Since the hospitals served as medical schools also, each hospital had a big lecture hall, in which lectures were delivered and practical education was imparted to the students as is done today in the hospitals attached to the medical colleges. The attendance of the students was compulsory in the hospitals. The conditions and diseases of the patients were also discussed and recorded. The books *al-Hawi* and *Kitab-ul-Fakhir* by al-Rãzî contain detailed descriptions of such clinical observations and treatments.

So much attention was paid to the care of the sleepless among the patients in some hospitals that they were provided with professional musicians, story-tellers and excellent reciters of the Qur'ãn. While the musicians and story-tellers entertained the patients with soft music, interesting stories and humorous anecdotes, the reciters of the Qur'ãn sought to stimulate their spiritual capacity with a view to solidifying their self-confidence. Besides, they were made to walk in the open air and given relaxing baths in order to mitigate their distress by relieving symptoms of tension. Of the numerous hospitals that spread throughout the Muslim world, the 'Adudî Hospital at Baghdad, the Nûrî Hospital at Damascus, the Mansûrî Hospital at Cairo and the Muwahhidî Hospital at Morocco were very famous.[12]

The endeavours made by Muslim physicians in fighting contagious diseases were also highly commendable and praiseworthy. They discovered and successfully treated a number of contagious diseases such as leprosy, tuberculosis, small-pox, measles, scabies, epidemic plague, etc. Ali Ibn Sahl al-Tabarî was the first Muslim physician who described the disease of leprosy in detail alongwith its symptoms such as deformation of the fingers, wrinkling of the nails and contraction of the nose. Ibn Sînã was another important physician who contributed a great deal to the study and treatment of this disease on scientific lines. He was also the first to give a minute description of the disease of tuberculosis, which, as described by him, mostly occurred in the age range of eighteen to thirty.

The credit for accurately distinguishing between the contagious diseases of small-pox and measles goes to Ibn Zakariya al-Rãzî. His book *al-Judarîyu w-al-Hasbah* (Small-pox and Measles) is one of the most outstanding books on this subject which was translated into Latin and other European languages and published more than forty times between 1498 and 1866. His most comprehensive medical work *al-Hãwî* in twenty volumes is too well-known to need any introduction. It was translated into

Latin under the title *Continens* which exerted a great influence on European medicine.

The Muslim physicians made successful attempts to fight the dreadful contagious disease of the plague also by describing the causes of its spread. It was clearly pointed out by the physician Lisãnuddin Ibn-ul-Khatîb that contagious diseases spread either through contact with the patient or through that with the dresses and utensils used by him. Air was also described by him as an active agent of spreading bacteria of such diseases. In view of this fact it is wrong to say as mentioned in the Encyclopedia Britannica (Vol. XV, p. 203) that "the first consistent explanation of the spread of disease by contagion was made by the Veronese physician Girolamo Fracastoro."

Surgery:

The Muslim contribution to surgery is best represented by Abul Qãsim al-Zahrãwî (936-1013 A.D.) of Cordova, who was a devoted surgeon, to whom both medical students and patients flocked from all parts of Europe and the Muslim world for advice and treatment. His claim to fame rests on his medical encyclopedia titled *al-Tasrif*. This book is divided into thirty sections, in the last of which he has summed up the surgical knowledge of his time. It also contains illustrations of about 200 surgical instruments, most of which the author had designed and developed himself. The surgical part of the book was early translated into Latin by Gerard of Cremona. Later, it was translated into Hebrew, French and English. Various editions of it were published at Venice in 1497, at Basel in 1541 and at Oxford in 1778. It was considered so indispensable for medical students in those days that the famous French surgeon Guy de Chauliac (1300-1368 A.D.) appendd its Latin version to his own book on surgery.

In short, al-Zahrãwî made numerous researches and inventions which helped lay the foundations of surgery on modern lines. He introduced such new ideas as cauterization of wounds, crushing a stone inside the bladder, etc. He was the first to have used thread of silk for stitching wounds. He also performed caesarean operations and wrote in detail about them. Besides, oral surgery and dentistry were highly developed by him.[13]

Psychotherapy:

Psychotherapy which is generally taken to be a recently developed branch of modern medicine was highly developed by Muslim physicians. Some of them specialized in it and made a systematic study of psychological diseases and their treatment. Ali Bin Sahl al-Tabarî (d. 861 A.D.), author of the earliest Arabic book on medicine titled *Firdaws-ul-Hikmah*) (Paradise of Wisdom), described psychological diseases as diseases of the head that are generally caused by mental disorders consequent upon psychological factors such as grief, anger, *ishq* (love), etc. He has suggested that such diseases can be cured by removing the causes of anger and insecurity to the patient as well as pacifying his heart with pleasant conversations congenial to his ethos.

Ishãq Bin 'Imrãn (d. 908 A.D.) was another eminent Muslim author who wrote an independent book on the disease of melancholia which he has described to be both acquired and herditary.

Ibn Zakariya al-Rãzî wrote a separate book on psychotherapy under the title *al-Tibb-ul-Ruhani* in which, he has thrown sufficient light on the methods, scope and application of psychiatric medicine by pointing out the close relationship between psyche and soma. He revealed that even indigestion is preceded by psychological upheavals in the body. Psychological conditions, according to this physician, have always the upper hand in regulating health because the ethos of the body is governed by the impact of such conditions dominating the mind. On the basis of this argument he held that only a competent psychotherapist could become a successful physician.

Ibn Sînã (d. 1038 A.D.) was another important physician who contributed a great deal to the development of psychotherapy. His medical encyclopedia *The Canon* remained the supreme authority on medicine for about six centuries not only in the Muslim world, but also in the Christian West. He was the first physician to clearly point out that much of natural disposition of the mother is diffused into her children through breast-feeding. He therefore, advised that the breast-feeding mother should keep herself on a high level of morality for the sake of the child.

In addition to the above, there were numerous other physicians who excelled in this branch of medical treatment. Although it is not possible to enumerate the achievements of all of them, a passing reference to the remaining eminent of them is given below.

Ibn-ul-Jazzãr Ahmad Bin Ibrahim (d. 1005 A.D.), author of many books, in which he disseminated his vast knowledge of psychotherapy including the management and care of children right from the moment of their conception in the womb to the stage of their adolescence; Ali Bin Ridwãn (d. 1067 A.D.), author of *al-Kifãyah f-il-Tibb*, in which he has illustrated the point that the beating of the heart is closely related with the psychological conditions of the mind; Hibatullah Ab-ul-Barakat, who flourished in Baghdad in the twelfth century, and Ibn Zuhr (d. 1162 A.D.) of Muslim Spain[14] have dealt with a number of psychological diseases in their medical works.

Anatomy:

The glaring achievements of the Muslims in the science of anatomy are generally dismissed by European historians on the assumption that since they were forbidden by their religion to practice dissection of human bodies, they could not make any progress in anatomy, and consequently medical science never went beyond Galen under them. But the fact is that there is nothing in Islam which may be interpreted to be a ban on the dissection of human bodies for medical purposes. It is, of course, true that mutilation of the dead body is forbidden in Islam in the light of the Prophet's saying: "Refrain from mutilating the body." But that is altogether in a different context. There is evidence to show that the Muslim scientists performed anatomy not only on animals but also on human bodies.

The Muslim scientists thoroughly analyzed the Greek legacy to anatomy and enriched it with their own contributions. Al-Jahiz, Yuhanna Ibn Māsawayh, Mansûr Ibn Muhammad, 'Abdul Latif al-Baghdadi, Ali Ibn 'Abbas and Hunayn Ibn Ishaq greatly advanced our knowledge of the anatomical structure of the different parts of the human body, specially the skull, the ear and the eye.

Another crowning achievement in the field of anatomy was made by Ibn al-Nafīs (1210-1288 A.D.), personal physician of the Mamluk Sultan ZahirBaybars, hero of the crusade wars. He minutely and scientifically described the lungs and the blood circulation about three centuries ahead of Willam Harvey who is erroneously credited with having been the first discoverer of it. He was also the first to notice that the heart has blood vessels inside its muscles. As regards the blood circulation of the heart, it was described by the Spanish Arab physician Ibn Rushd in his *al-Kulliyāt*.[15]

Zoology and Veterinary Medicine:

Islam inspired the early Muslims to develop a strong interest in the kingdom of animals also by describing them as organised and intelligent creatures that deserve proper attention and kind treatment. They now paid special attention to the care, feeding, breeding and scientific study of them. A number of Muslim scientists flourished who made systematic studies on animals, wrote books on them, and thus contributed a great deal to the science of zoology ad veterinary medicine.

Al-Jãhiz (d. 869 A.D.) was the first eminent Arab Zoologist. His *Kitãb-ul-Hayawãn* is a systematic and comprehensive study of animals. In it he has described in detail the kinds of animals, their behavioural characteristics and their diseases and treatment. This encyclopedic work in seven big volumes, in which he has quoted and criticised Aristotle at several places, proved a very useful contribution on the history of natural science. It also contained germs of the later theories of evolution, adaptation and animal psychology.[16] The chief contribution of the author in this book lies in the fact that, besides tapping almost all the extant sources of knowledge on animal life, specially Arabic and Greek, he has provided a great deal of fresh scientific information from his own observations and experiments as well as the discussions which he held with those who had first-hand knowledge about animals as sailors and hunters. It is a well-known fact that he used to slaughter animals for studying the internal parts of their bodies. He also opened the belly of the pregnant animal to find out the number of embryos and the position of each one of them in the body. Besides, he has thrown light on the changes that occur in birds through migrations and on the life history of bees and locusts.

The Egyptian philosopher-theologian Kamaluddin al-Damiri (d. 1405 A.D.) was the next important author on this subject. Greatly influenced by al-Jahiz, he became the greatest Arab zoologist. His book *Hiyãt-ul-Hayawãn* (Life of Animals), arranged in the alphabetical order, contains a mine of curious information on animal life and natural science. Al-Masudî, Ibn Sinã, Ibn Rushd and the *Ikhwãn-ul-Safa* (the Brethren of Purity) were other eminent Muslim writers who made significant contributions to zoology.

Vesterinary medicine developed side by side with the cultivation of zoological studies. It is worthy of mention in this context that special attention was paid to the study of horses as well as their diseases and treatment. It was developed almost to the rank of an independent science. The first systematic book on this subject was written by Muhammad Akhi Hizam around 860 A.D. It deals in detail with different aspects of horsemanship and related matters.

The book *al-Mukhassas* by Ibn Sîdah (d. 1066 A.D.) was another significant contribution in this field. Written in the form of a dictionary, it discusses the characteristics of camels, goats, sheep, birds, wild animals, etc., as well as the diseases that afflict them. It also contains information about useful and harmful insects. It was printed in seventeen volumes at the Bulaq Press in Egypt.

But the greatest medieval work on veterinary science is the comprehensive manual *Kãmil-ul-Sinã'a taynf-il-Baytarah w-al-Zardaqah* by Abu Bakr al-Baytar of Cairo (d. 1340 A.D.), who was the incharge of the stable of the Mamluk Sultan Muhammad al-Nãsir Bin Qalãwûn. It covers a wide range of topics including animal behaviour, husbandry, breeding, variations in wild and domestic animals, horsemanship and related matters.[17] It contains a specialized and detailed study on animal diseases in different seasons, specially those of horses, and on the methods of their prevention and treatment with drugs. A separate chapter is devoted to the discussion of determining the age of horses with the mention of their anatomical characteristics. Divided into ten sections, this book is a voluminous work which contains the sum total of the medieval Arab knowledge of veterinary medicine.

An idea of the success achieved by the Muslims in animal husbandry and veterinary medicine may be derived from the huge quantities of animal produce under their management. The period in which the Mamluk Sultan Muhammad al-Nãsir Bin Qalawûn ruled was the most notable for the breeding of animals on scientific lines. The Sultan was very fond of horses and cattle. He even established a farm at his castle in 714 A.H. When he died in 741 A.H., there were as many as eighty thousand cattle in it. Besides, as reported by al-Maqrîzzi, over eighty thousand cattle were slaughtered annually from that farm. Similarly, Sultãn al-Malik-al-Zãhir Burûq had a great interest in the breeding of animals. He is said to have left behind at his castle twelve thousand horses, five thousand camels and an equal number of mules. That was in addition to the large numbers of cattle that were slaughtered from his farm for daily consumption.

Obviously, the fruitful breeding of domestic animals on such a wide scale could not have been possible except with the efficient services of competent veterinary physicians and skilled workers.

Botany and Agriculture:

The contribution made by the Muslims in botany and agriculture are also very valuable. The Greek and Nabataean legacies together with the indigenous traditions formed the basis of their botanical and agricultural knowledge. A number of Muslim scientists flourished who devoted themselves to systematic studies of plants and their cultivation, and wrote several detailed manuals on the subject which in the course of time became the main source material for the development of modern botanical and agricultural sciences. Jãbir Ibn Hayyãn, Abu Zayd al-Ansãrî, Ibn-ul-Sikkît, Abu Sa'd al-Asma'î, Abû Hanîfah al-Dînawarî, al-Ghãfiqî, Ibn-ul-Baytãr were noted botanists, while Ibn Wahshiyah, Ibn-ul-'Awwãm, etc., were distinguished agricultural scientists.

Of the early Arab authors who wrote on plant life, Abu Hanîfah al-Dînawarî (d. 895 A.D.) deserves special mention. His *Kitab-ul-Nabãt* on botany in six volumes is massive in size and rich in contents of which unfortunately only volumes 3 and 6 and fragments of the fourth could be preserved.[18] It covers the classification of plants in general and the morphological structure of the individual plants in three groups-plants cultivated for food, fruit-bearing plants and wild plants.[19] In all he has described 1120 plants. It is an authentic source of information about the medicinal plants also that were known in pre-Islamic Arabia. It is rightly regarded as the first most comprehensive work upon medicae materiae.[20]

It goes to the credit of al-Dînawarî that he has thrown sufficient light on plant sex life-the phenomenon which is generally taken to be a recent discovery of modern science. An idea of his sharp observation on this vital aspect of plant life may be derived from the following quotation:

> "Date-palm is so near to animals and even to human beings that sometimes there are love-affairs: sometimes a female date-palm gets amorous of a certain male date-palm. The female tree even physically inclines towards its beloved. If the gardener pollinates this famale palm with the pollens of some male palm other than its beloved one, it does not bear fruit, and gets sick until the gardener discovers its beloved tree and "marries them" by sprinkling the pollens of that particular male palm."[21]

Ibn-ul-Baytãr (d. 1249 A.D.), who flourished in Muslim Spain wrote the most comprehensive book on botany under the title *al-Jãmi' li-Mufradãt-il-Adwiyah w-al-Aghdhiyah* which remained the most important encyclopedia on this subject upto the sixteenth century. It contains the descriptions of more than 1400 medicinal plants and herbs.

This author elaborated for the first time the impact of storage on the nourishing elements of the plants. The discovery made by him in this field played an important role in evolving the scientific methods of storing and preserving medicinal and aromatic plants.

Ibn Wahshîyah (d. 909 A.D.), author of about thirty books, was a great agronomist. His most famous work titled *al-Filãhat-ul-Nabatîyah* (The Nabataean Agriculture) covers a variety of subjects on applied agricultural sciences. For example, one chapter is devoted to the discussion of the properties of the olive, while another chapter deals with the science of choosing suitable places for digging wells in order to procure sufficient quantities of water for the purpose of irrigation. The book contains valuable information regarding cultivation of various crops, fruits and vegetables. It also deals with the methods of fighting the diseases and calamities that befall standing crops and plants. It proved so useful and indispensable that it was consulted by almost all the later Muslim authors who wrote on this subject.

Ibn-ul-'Awwãm was another important agricultural scientist. But he remained neglected for a long time. His *Kitãb-ul-Filãhah* was first edited with a Latin translation in 1802 by J.A. Banqueri; while E. Meyer gave a summary of it in his *Geschichte der Botanik.* Its French translation was published by Clement-Mullet in 1864.[22]

Divided into thirty-four chapters, this book covers in detail a variety of subjects like species of plants, medicinal and aromatic plants, farming techniques, seasons and methods of cultivation of different crops, fruits and vegetables, irrigation, etc. He was the first to write on what is known today as the technology of soil. He also paid attention to what is known today as seed testing and agricultural industries technology.[23]

Exact and Other Sciences:

Now a few words about some spectacular achievements made by Muslim scientists in other fields, specially exact sciences, may not be out of place here. The names of al-Khwarizmî, the sons of Mûsã, al-Battãni, al-Bîrunî, Ibn-ul-Haytham, Nasîruddin al-Tûsî, etc., are very famous for cultivation of exact sciences in Islam. Of them Ibn-ul-Haytham and Nasîruddin al-Tûsî deserve special mention in this context.

Ibn-ul-Haytham (965-1039 A.D.), one of the greatest physicists of all time, made valuable experimental contributions in optics. Contrary to the Greek concept of vision, he presented a correct theory of the process of visual perception, according to which vision occurs when light emanating form the seen object enters the eye. As described by Professor Muhammad Abdus Salam, he anticipated Fermat's Principle of Least Time by many centuries by enunciating that a ray of light, in passing through a medium, takes the easier and quicker path. He also enunciated the law of inertia which later became Newton's first law of motion.[24]

As regards Nasîruddin al-Tûsî, he made substantial progress in trigonometry and planetary astronomy. It was mainly through his efforts that trigonometry became an independent branch of mathematics. His most original work on this subject is titled as *Kitãb-ul-Shakl-il-Qattã*'. It was later translated into Latin, English and French, upon which the Europeans depended for a long time for their knowledge of trigonometry.

Another important achievement of al-Tûsî was that he and his colleagues at the Maraghah Observatory considerably advanced the knowledge of planetary astronomy. He produced better planetary models which had a great similarity with those of the Polish astronomer Nicolaus Copernicus. His book *Tadhkirah fi 'Ilm-il-Hay'at* contains a survey of the whole field of astronomy. In it he has criticised Ptolemy for his views expressed in the *Almagest*. It was this criticism which enabled Copernicus to enunciate his theory of the celestial bodies which had far-reaching implications for the rise of modern science.[25]

Lastly, the Muslims achieved distinctions in chemistry, oceanography, mineralogy, geology, mechanical technology, etc., produced books on them, and made significant contributions to the progress of civilization.

It is sufficiently clear from the above that the lofty achievements and performances of modern science in almost all its branches have deep roots in the studies and researches made by the Arabs and Muslims which cannot be neglected while making a survey of the history of science and civilization.

Finally, please permit me to close these observations with due stress on the point that there is a growing need for the promotion of studies and research on the scientific foundations of Islam as well as intellectual contributions of the Muslims not only to give them their rightful place in the history of science and civilization, but also to present to the modern people the genuine image of Islam as a mission for the welfare of humanity at large, thereby adequately reflecting the chief ingredients of its dynamism.

I thank you once again for the patient hearing you have so kindly given to me and honour you have done me by electing me to preside over the deliberations of the Islamic Studies Section for the second time.

NOTES AND REFERENCES

1. The Qur'ãn, XCIX:7-8.
2. The Qur'ãn, II:269 (tr. by M.M. Pickthall).
3. The Qur'ãn, LVIII:11.
4. The Qur'ãn, IV:135.
5. Professor Abdus Salam: "Islam and Science" in *Hamdard Medicus*, Pakistan, Vol. XXIX, No. 4, p. 3.
6. *Ibid.*, p. 4.
7. The Qur'ãn, XV:22.
8. M.M. Pickthall, *Cultural Side of Islam*, p. 68.
9. The Qur'ãn, XXXVI:36.
10. The Qur'ãn, XXI:33 (tr. by M.M. Pickthall).
11. For details see "Care of Health in Islam" by Abdul Ali in *Hamdard Medicus*, Vol. XXIX, No. 4 (October-December 1986), pp. 53-70.
12. For details see "The Arab Hospital System in the Middle Ages" by Abdul Ali in *The Muslim World League Journal*, Saudi Arabia, Vol. XII, Nos. 9&10 (June-July 1985), pp. 27-29.
13. For details see "Al-Zahrawi - One of the Greatest Arab Surgeons of Medieval Times" by Abdul Ali in *Islam Today*, Morocco, No. 2, 1984, pp. 61-64.
14. For details see "Medical Services of the Banu Zuhr Family" by Abdul Ali in *The Muslim World League Journal*, Vol. XVII, Nos. 3&4, pp. 18-20.
15. For details see "Arab Legacy to the Science of Anatomy" by Abdul Ali in *Islam Today*, No. 4, 1986, pp. 28-32.
16. P.K. Hitti, *History of the Arabs,* p. 382.
17. *The Genius of Arab Civilization*, edited by Sami K. Hamarneh, p. 183.

18. Muhammad Hamidullah: "Early Muslim Contribution to Botany" in the Journal *Al-'Ilm*, Durban, Vol. 5 (January 1985), p. 9.
19. E.J. Brill, *First Encyclopedia of Islam*, Vol. II, p. 978.
20. Hakim Muhammad Said: "Islamic Medicine and the Art of Drug Making - A Historical Perspective" in *Hamdard Medicus*, Vol. XXXIII, No. 1, 1990, p. 47.
21. Muhammad Hamidullah, *op.cit.*, p. 9.
22. *First Encyclopedia of Islam*, Vol. III, p. 365.
23. Dr. Ali al-Majdoub: "*Al-Zir'atu w-al-Baytarah 'ind-al-Muslimin*" in the Journal *al-Islam-ul-Yawm,* 1983, Morocco, No. 1, p. 58.
24. Professor Muhammad Abdus Salam, *op.cit.*, p. 5.
25. For details see the article "Nasîruddin al-Tûsî" (in Arabic) by Dr. Abdul Azim Anis in the Journal *al-Arabi*, Kuwait, No. 330 (May 1986), pp. 37-39.

PRESIDENTIAL ADDRESS: ARABIC AND PERSIAN SECTION,

37th Session, A.I.O.C., Rohtak (1994)

Fellow Delegates and Distinguished Scholars,

Let me begin my address by expressing my gratefulness to you for having given me the honour of presiding over the Arabic and Persian Section of the Conference. I trust that with your co-operation I shall be able to perform the duties assigned to me to the satisfaction of all concerned.

First of all, I crave your indulgence for departing from the usual review-type address on this occasion. As a student of Arabic studies I would rather like to emphasize upon you the importance of the hitherto little-studied role played by the numerous post-Abbasid Arab and Persian dynasties in the advancement of science and civilization by taking up in my address the treatment of a particular topic relating to a neglected area of research in this context.

It is an historical fact that the decline of the Abbasid Caliphate in the Arab East and of the Umayyad Caliphate in Muslim Spain gave rise to numerous major and minor dynasties in both eastern and western wings of the medieval Arab world. Some of these dynasties generously patronised and carried on the traditions of Arab-Islamic learning and culture on a wide scale, thereby maintaining a continuity in Muslim contributions to the advancement of science and civilization.

But it is a matter of deep regret that while comparatively sufficient work has been done on various aspects of the literary, scientific and cultural heritage of the Arabs under the Umayyads and the Abbasids, the contributions made by these lesser dynasties have not yet been properly studied and analyzed. It is mainly for this reason that this address is devoted to an assessment of the scientific and literary progress made under the Syro-Egyptian Mamluk Dynasty (1250-1517 C.E.), which is perhaps the most significant from the viewpoint of its intellectual and artistic contributions. It is hoped that this will not only serve a useful purpose in tracing and bringing to light the continuity in Arab-Muslim contributions to the advancement of scientific knowledge, but also inspire Arabic and Persian scholars to pay more attention to this important area of study and research.

It is worthy of mention here that when the Mamluks captured power from the Ayyubids, they had their own compulsions and priorities. It certainly goes to their credit that they not only stopped for ever the further advance of the invincible Mongols by inflicting a crushing defeat upon them in the historic battle of Ayn Jalut in 1260 C.E., but also completed the unfinished task of the Ayyubids by ousting the Crusaders out of Muslim Asia.

But despite all their preoccupation with the unavoidable military campaigns, the Mamluk sultans are credited with having generously patronised and encouraged intellectual and artistic pursuits, as a result of which there flourished in this period a good number of intellectual and literary giants, the like of whom both in number and quality is hard to find elsewhere in the post-Abbasid era. Their main scientific and literary achievements are briefly assessed below.

Medicine

The Sultans took keen interest in the development of medicine. The magnificent Mansuri Hospital built by Sultan Qalawun in Cairo may be taken as an index of their interest in medicine as well as of the high level of medical care provided to the patients.

The Mansuri Hospital was the greatest of its time. It had an endowment which yielded about a million dirhams annually. Both male and female attendants were employed in it. Within a spacious quadrangular enclosure four high walls were raised in cruciform round a pillared courtyard with the inbuilt system of keeping it cooled with fountains and brooks. Of the four halls, one was set apart for the hospital staff, and the other three for the patients.

Sultan Qalawun is said to have received inspiration for starting construction of this hospital while lying ill with colic pain at the Nûrî Hospital in Damascus, where he had vowed to establish a similar institution in Cairo in the event of his recovery. The structure of the hospital including its annexes as well as a school and a mosque, was completed in 1284 C.E. The entire art of that age was employed to make the stay of the patients there comfortable, pleasant and cheerful.[1]

So much attention was paid to the care of the sleepless among the patients at this hospital that the call to prayer was sounded two hours earlier than its usual time, to make the night appear shorter to those who could not sleep.[2]

Likewise, the Mamluk period saw the rise of some eminent physicians and surgeons, who contributed a great deal to the development of medical science. Their achievements are briefly introduced below.

Ibn-ul-Nafîs

The dean of the Mansuri Hospital, Ibn-ul-Nafîs, was the greatest medical scientist of his time and one of the greatest of all times. He was also the personal physician of the Mamluk ruler al-Zãhir Baybars al-Bundûqdãrî (ruled 1260-1277 C.E.), hero of the Crusade wars. An idea of the excellence of this physician may be had from the fact that he criticised both Galen and Ibn Sina, and corrected them on several points.

The medical writings of Ibn-ul-Nafîs comprise both original works and commentaries on the books of his predecessors, in which he gave sufficient proof of his bold and independent approach in the cause of the advancement of medical knowledge.

His commentaries include *Sharh-ul-Fusûl* and *Sharhu Taqdimat-il-Ma'rifah* by Hippocrates; *Sharh-ul-Masã'il* by Hunayn Ibn Ishãq; *Sharh-ul-Qãnûn* in four volumes. (1) *Sharhu Kullîyãt-il-Qãnûn*, (2) *Sharh-ul-Adwiyat-il-Basîtah w-al-Murakkabah*, (3) *Sharh-ul-Amrãd min al-Ra'si il-al-Qadam*, (4) *Sharhul Amrãd illatî lã takhtassu li 'Udwin dûna ghayrih* - and *Sharhu Tashrîh-il-Qãnûn* by Ibn Sina.

He also wrote a resume of the *Qãnûn* under the title *al-Mu'jiz*, which became very popular in medical circles throughout the world. It was translated into a number of languages including Hebrew and Turkish, and published several times. It was published in India also at the Naval Kishore Press, Lucknow, in August 1877 C.E.

As regards the original works of Ibn-ul-Nafîs on general medicine, the following books are very famous:

Al-Shãmil f-il-Tibb

This is the most voluminous of his books. Originally, he had planned to produce it as an encyclopedia of medicine in 300 volumes. But he could not fulfil this plan due to his advanced age. When he died, only 80 volumes were completed, most of which are now unfortunately lost into oblivion.

Al-Mukhtãr min-al-Aghdhiyah

This is an original book on the effects of diet on health. It also contains guidelines regarding prescription of suitable diets to sick persons.

Ibn-ul-Nafîs as Discoverer of Blood Circulation

Although all the medical works of Ibn-ul-Nafîs have great scientific value, his title to fame rests on his *Sharhu Tashrîh-il-*

Qãnûn, in which he is credited with having discovered and scientifically described the system of blood circulation in the human body about three centuries ahead of William Harvey. The relevant passages embodying the findings of his research on the subject are translated below in support of this point:

> "The heart has two ventricles. The right ventricle is full of blood, while the left is full of purified blood. And there is no direct passage of blood between these two ventricles, because the cardiac septum is quite thick.
>
> "The passage of blood from the right ventricle to the left takes place through the lungs where blood sent by the heart from its right ventricle is mixed with air, and then returned to the left ventricle...."[3]

It is quite evident from the above that Ibn-ul-Nafis must have performed anatomy on a number of dead human bodies, of which there was no dearth in the time of his patron al-Zãhir Baybars, who killed large numbers of enemy soldiers in the Crusade wars. Thus he deserves to be honoured not only as discoverer of the pulmonary blood circulation, but also as promoter of our knowledge about the functions of the hearts, lungs and arteries.[4]

Ibn-ul-Quff

Ibn-ul-Quff (1233-1285 C.E.), was the greatest surgeon of his time. His book *al-'Umdah fi Sinã'at-il-Jirãhah* or *'Umdat-ul-Jarrãhîn* (The Support of Surgeons) was the first Arabic text exclusively devoted to the art of surgery, which contains a comprehensive description of surgical operations and bodily injuries. In it he has explained "the functions of the capillaries - the minute blood passages that connect arteries and veins - and the action of cardiac valves in the veins and in the heart chambers, describing how they open in only one direction to keep blood flowing in the same way".[5] His another important book on preservation of health and treatment of diseases is titled as *Jãmi-ul-Gharad fi Hifz-il-Sihhah wa Daf'-il-Marad.*

Ibn Abî Usaybi'ah

He was also an eminent physician and medical author, who flourished in the early Mamluk period. Having received his elementary education at home, he completed his medical training at the Nãsirî Hospital in Cairo. He is particularly famous for his masterpiece *'Uyûn-ul-Anbã fi Tabaqãt-il-Atibbã* (Fountains of Information on the Classes of Physicians), which is a collection of about four hundred biographies of Arab and Greek medical men. Since most of these physicians were distinguished philosophers and scientists also, the book serves as an invaluable source for the history of Arab science in general.[6]

Other Eminent Authors on Medicine

In addition to the above, there were numerous other physicians and authors who flourished under the Mamluks. The notable among them were the Jewish pharmacist of Egypt, al-Kûhîn al-'Attãr, author of *Minhãj-ul-Dukkãn wa Dastûr-ul-A'yãn* (A Manual for Official Drugs and a Canon for Notables); Salãhuddîn Hibatullah, author of *al-Irsh ãd li Masãlih-il-Anfãs w-al-Ajsãd* (Instructions in the Health of Souls and Bodies)[7]; and Muhammad al-Qawsawî, author of *Kamãl-ul-Farhah fi Daf'-il-Sumûm wa Hifz-il-Sihhah* on treatment of the effects of poison and maintenance of health.[8]

Ophthalmology

Ophthalmology was another important branch of medicine which made significant progress under the Mamluk rule. Special attention was paid to its development because of the high incidence of eye diseases in Syria and Egypt. The two most significant books on the subject were *al-Kãfi f-il-Kuhl* (The Sufficient Work on Collyrium) by Khalîfah Ibn Ab-il-Mahãsin, who flourished in Aleppo about 1256 C.E.; and *Nûr-ul-'Uyûn wa Jãmi'-ul-Funûn* (Light of the Eyes and Compendium of Arts) by Salãhuddîn bin Yûsuf, who practised in Hamah about 1296 C.E. Khalîfah Ibn Ab-il-Mahãsin was a very expert eye surgeon of his time. He was so confident of his skill that once he operated even upon a one-eyed patient to remove a cataract without any hesitation.[9]

Another valuable and comprehensive work on ophthalmology was written by the above-mentioned physician, Ibn-ul-Nafîs, under the title *al-Muhadhdhab fi Hikmat-il-'Ayn* (The Fine Book on Ophthalmology). Several manuscripts of this book are preserved in the libraries of Damascus, Istanbul, Berlin and Vatican. It is divided into two parts preceded by a preface. The preface comprising three sections deals in detail with the scope of opthalmology, the anatomical structure of the eye in respect of different animals as well as with the specialities of man in the matter of the eye. The first part is devoted to the discussion of the general guidelines which the oculists ought to know, while the second part deals with the fundamentals and particulars of the oculist science. The book discusses, among numerous eye diseases, the causes and methods of cure of the disease of strabismus.[10]

Veterinary Science and Animal Husbandry

Abû Bakr Ibn-ul-Mundhir al-Baytãr (d. 1340 C.E.), was the greatest veterinary scientist of the Middle Ages, who served as groom of the stable of Sultan al-Nãsir Muhammad bin Qalãwûn. His excellent and comprehensive book on the subject bore the title *Kãmil-ul-Sinã'atayn f-il-Baytarah w-al-Zardaqah*, which is known after the name of his patron as *al-Nãsirî* also. It covers a wide range of topics including animal behaviour, husbandry, breeding, variations in wild and domestic animals, horsemanship and related matters. It contains a specialised and detailed study on animal diseases in different seasons, especially those of horses, and on the methods of their prevention and treatment with drugs. A separate chapter is devoted to the discussion of determining the age of horses along with the mention of the characteristics of different parts of their bodies.

Divided into ten sections, the book is a voluminous work which contains the sum total of the medieval Arab knowledge of veterinary science. It was translated by M. Perron with a full introduction. The first volume, which appeared in 1852, is introductory and contains a wealth of information about the Arabian horses as well as Sultan al-Nãsir's particular services to horse-breeding in Egypt. The second volume (1859) is the translation of the hippology, while the third volume (1860) contains translation of the hippiatry.[11]

Abdul Mu'min al-Dimyãtî (1217-1306), a lecturer at the Mansuriyah Academy of Qalawun, was another eminent author on the subject. His book *Fadl-ul-Khayl* (Excellence of the Horse) is a very useful contribution in this field.

An idea of the success achieved by the Arabs of this period in veterinary science and animal husbandry may be derived from the big quantities of animal produce under their management. The reign of Sultan al-Nãsir Muhammad bin Qalawun was the most notable for the breeding of animals on scientific lines, who was very fond of horses and cattle. He even established a farm at his castle with only 2000 cattle in 714/1313. But when he died in 741/1340, there were as many as 80,000 cattle in his farm. Besides, about 80,000 cattle were slaughtered annually from that farm. Similarly, Sultan al-Zahir Barquq was also equally interested in the breeding of animals. He is said to have left behind him 12,000 horses, 5000 camels and an equal number of mules. And that was in addition to the large numbers of cattle that were slaughtered from his farm for daily consumption.[12]

Obviously, the fruitful breeding of domestic animals on such a wide scale could not have been possible except with the efficient services of competent veterinary physicians and skilled workers.

Zoology

The Mamluk period also saw the rise of the greatest Arab zoologist, Kamãluddîn al-Damîrî (d. 1405 C.E.). Greatly influenced by al-Jãhiz, he produced his masterpiece under the title *Hayãt-ul-Hayawãn* (The Animal Life). In it he has arranged and discussed animals in the alphabetical order and dealt in detail with their characteristics, qualities and habits. He has also pointed out the medicinal values of their organs as mentioned in folk medicine.[13]

Mathematics and Astronomy

Contrary to the popular view that after the middle of the thirteenth century leadership in mathematics and astronomy was maintained mainly by Arabic-speaking Persian scholars, who worked at the Îlkhãnid observatory and library of Marãghah,[14] the Mamluk period also produced a number of illustrious mathematicians and astronomers, whose works cannot be neglected while making an assessment of Arab-Muslim intellectual legacy.

Ibn-ul-Hã'im

Ahmad bin Muhammad, know to fame as Ibn-ul-Hã'im (1352-1412 C.E.), was the greatest mathematician of the Mamluk period. He wrote a number of valuable books and treatises on arithmetic and algebra. His *al-Luma' f-il-Hisãb* is a very important treatise on arithmetic. The book is divided into three chapters preceded by a preface. The first chapter is devoted to the discussion of various methods of multiplication of different numbers. In it he has illustrated with examples several formulas of multiplication of certain particular numbers in an easy and swift manner without going through the usual procedure of multiplication. To quote his own words: "Every number which is multiplied with 15 or 150 or 1500, half its number should be added to it, and the sum total should be expanded with tens or hundreds or thousands respectively. For example, if you are asked to multiply 24 with 15, add to 24 half its number, and then expand its sum total (24+12=36) with tens. So the answer will be 360. Similarly, if you are asked to multiply 24 with 150, expand the sum total of 24 and its half (24+12=36) with hundreds, and the answer will be 3,600...."[15]

The second chapter of the book deals with the methods of division of different kinds of numbers, while the third chapter comprising four sections discusses fractions of numbers. The language and style of the book is simple and scientific. It has been acclaimed by scholars as a rich storehouse of mathematical knowledge.

His other important books are *al-Ma'ûnah f-il-Hisãb-il-Hawã'ĩ* on arithmetic; *al-Wasîlah* on arithmetic; *Ghãyat-ul-Su'l f-il-Iqrãr b-il-Majhûl* on arithmetic and algebra; *Kitãbun Hãwin f-il-Hisãb;* and *al-Muqanna'* which is an ode containing fifty-two verses on algebra.[16]

Other Eminent Mathematicians and Astronomers

Of the numerous other mathematicians and astronomers of this period, Ibn-ul-Shãtir (1304-1379-80 C.E.) and Ibn Tîbûghã al-Qãhirî (1359-1447 C.E.) deserve special mention here.

Ibn-ul-Shãtir was the author of a number of books on astronomy, trigonometry and mathematical tables. His *al-Ashi' 'at-ul-Lãmi'ah* is very important. Arranged into thirty chapters and a conclusion preceded by a preface, it was used as an invaluable reference book on mathematical sciences. A summarised version of the book is also available under the title *al-Thimãr-ul-Yãni'ah fi Qutûf-il-Ãlat-il-Jãmi'ah.*[17]

Similarly, Ibn Tîbûghã al-Qãhirî was also a prolific author on astronomy, arithmetic, trigonometry and mathematical tables. His *Khulãsat-ul-Aqwãl fi Ma'rifat-il-Waqt wa Ru'yat-il-Hilãl* on the measuring of time and the sighting of the new moon, was one of the best books of its time on the subject. Some of his books are preserved in the libraries of Leiden, Oxford and Cairo.[18]

Biographical and Historical Literature

This period was quite fertile for the production of biographical books. Some of the most famous and earliest works on the subject were produced under the Mamluks. Shamsuddîn Ahmad bin Muhammad Ibn Khallikãn (1211-1282 C.E.) wrote his masterpiece *Wafayãt-ul-A'yãn wa Anbã'u Abnã'-il-Zamãn* (Deaths of Eminent Men and Historical Accounts of Distinguished Contemporaries), which is the first accurate and authentic collection of 865 biographies of prominent Muslims. It is rightly adjudged as "the best general biography ever written".[19]

Inspired by Ibn Khallikãn, two more authors produced important biographical works on the pattern of the above book. Of them Muhammad bin Shãkir bin Ahmad al-Kutubî (d. 1363) supplemented the work of his predecessor with the addition of 572 biographies under the title *Fawãt-ul-Wafayãt*. He was also the author of *'Uyûn-ul-Tawãrîkh* in six volumes.[20] While Salãhuddîn al-Safadî (1296-1363 C.E.) wrote his *al-Wãfî b-il-Wafayãt* comprising 14,000 biographies.[21] Other notable biographical works of this period were *al-Durar-ul-Kãminah fi 'Ulamã'-il-Mi'at-il-Thãminah* by Ibn Hajar al-'Asqalãnî (d. 1449 C.E.); and *al-Daw'-ul-Lãmi' fi 'Ulamã'-il-Qarn-il-Tãsi'* by Muhammad bin 'Abdul Rahmãn al-Sakhãwî (1427-1497 C.E.).

Likewise, the Mamluk period gave birth to a number of eminent historians, who compiled both local and universal histories.

The most prominent of them was Taqîy-ul-Dîn Ahmad al-Maqrîzî (1364-1442), who composed several standard works such as *al-Khitat* and *al-Sulûk*. His books contain a rich storehouse of authentic historical information, on account of which he has been admired by a Western Orientalist in the following words:

"He has accumulated and reduced to a certain amount of order a large quantity of information that would but for him have passed into oblivion. He is generally painstaking and accurate, and always resorts to contemporary evidence if it is possible. Also he has a pleasant and lucid style, and writes without bias and apparently with distinguished impartiality."[22]

Other eminent historians of this period were Abul Fidã (1273-1332 C.E.), author of *Mukhtasar Tãrîkh-il-Bashar* (Epitome of the History of Mankind); Ibn Fadlillãh al-'Umarî (1301-1349), author of *Masãlik-ul-Absãr fi Mamãlik-il-Amsãr* and *Mamãlik 'Ibãd-il-Salîb;* Al-Hãfiz Muhammad bin Ahmad al-Dhahabî (1274-1348), author of *Duwal-ul-Islãm*; Abul Mahãsin ibn Taghrîbirdî (1411-69), author of *al-Nujûm-ul-Zãhirah fi Mulûk Misr w-al-Qãhirah* on the history of Egypt from the Arab conquest till 1453; Jalãluddîn al-Suyûtî (1445-1505), author of *Husn-ul-Muhãdarah fi Akhbãr Misr w-al-Qãhirah* on the history of Egypt; and Ibn Iyãs (d. 1523), author of *Badã'i-'ul-Zuhûr fi Waqã'i'-il-Duhûr* on the history of Egypt.

Geographical Literature

In the field of geography the place of honour belongs to the above-mentioned historian-geographer Abul Fidã, whose *Taqwîm-ul-Buldãn* is an invaluable reference book on geographical knowledge about Iran and the Arab world. It also contains a gist of the geographical and astronomical findings of ancient scholars. It has been translated into a number of European languages.

Other main geographers were Shamsuddin al-Dimashqi (d. 1326), author of *Nukhbat-ul-Dahr fi 'Ajã'ib-il-Barr w-al-Bahr*; and Ahmad ibn Mãjid (d. after 1498), whose *Kitãb-ul-Fawã'id fi 'Usûl-il-Bahr w-al-Qawã'id* (The Book of Advantages on the Principles of Rulers of Oceanography) shows that he had studied the works of his predecessors on astronomical and mathematical geography. Ibn Mãjid is also credited with having piloted Vascoda Gama from Africa to India.[23]

In addition to the above, there flourished in this period two great encyclopedists. They are Ahmad al-Nuwayrî (d. 1332), author of *Nihãyat-ul-Arab fi Funûn-il-Adab*, which is a rich storehouse of knowledge on a variety of subjects of historical, literary and intellectual interests.; and Ahmad al-Qalaqshandî (d. 1418), whose *Subh-ul-A'shã* abounds in historical and geographical information about Egypt and Syria.[24]

Religious and Linguistic Literature

In the field of Islamic religious sciences the name of Ibn Taymiyah (1263-1328) is the most prominent. He was the greatest religious reformer of his time and one of the greatest of all times, who undertook the task of regenerating the Muslims by reviving the authentic, monotheistic aspects of the religion of Islam in accordance with the teachings of the Qur'ãn and the Apostolic Traditions. He also raised his voice against all sorts of un-Islamic practices and innovations that had crept into the religion in the course of time such as saint-worship, oblations and visits to shrines, etc. His best-known works are *Fatãwã Ibn Taymiyah*; *Muntaq-al-Akhbãr; al-Îmãn; al-Jam'u bayn-al-'Aql w-al-Naql; Minhãj-ul-Sunnat-il-Nabawîyah fi Naqd-il-Shî'ah w-al-Qadarîyah; al-Furqãn bayna Awliyã'illah wa Awliyã'il-Shaytãn; al-Wãsitah bayn-al-Haqq w-al-Khalq; al-Sãrim-ul-Maslûl 'ala Shãtim-il-Rasûl;* and *Majmu'-ul-Rasã'il-il-Kubrã.*

An idea of the importance of Ibn Taymiyah's books may be derived from the fact that about four centuries later they exerted a great impact upon Muhammad bin 'Abdul Wahhãb (d. 1792), who on his turn launched a successful revivalist movement in Central Arabia which became known in history as the Wahhãbî movement.

The above-mentioned Jalaluddîn al-Suyûtî was the next prominent author on Islamic studies and linguistics. His major works are *al-Itqãn fi 'Ulûm-il-Qur'ãn* on Qur'ãnic interpretation; *al-Muzhir fi 'Ulûm-il-Lughah* on Arabic philology, etc.

Other eminent authors on these subjects were Tãjuddiîn al-Subkî (1327-1370), author of *Tabaqãt-ul-Shãfi'îyat-il-Kubrã* in six volumes; *Shifã'-ul-Saqãm fi Ziyãrat Khayr-il-Anãm*, a critique on Ibn Taymiyah's thought; and *Jãmi'-ul-Jawãmi'* on the principles of jurisprudence; Ibn Hajar al-'Asqalãnî (1372-1449) author of *al-'Isãbah fi Tãrîkh-il-Sahãbah*, on history of the Companions of Prophet Muhammad (P.B.U.H.); *Fath-ul-Bãrî* on interpretation of the Apostolic Traditions compiled in the *Sahîh* of al-Bukhãrî, etc., and Mahmûd bin Ahmad al-'Aynî (1361-1451), author of *'Umdat-ul-Qãrî fi Sharh-il-Bukhãrî* in eleven volumes; *Maghãn-il-Akhyãr fi Rijãli Ma'ãn-il-Ãthãr* on technical terms of *Hadîth* and its men in two volumes; *al-Binãyah fi Sharh-il-Hidãyah* on the Hanafite jurisprudence in six volumes; *al-Maqãsid-ul-Nahwîyah*, etc.

Books on Warfare and Hunting

A number of books on different aspects of warfare such as military techniques, horse-racing, management of the army, sieging tactics, swordcraft, shooting of arrows, etc., were also produced in this period. Some eminent authors on these subjects were 'Imãduddîn Mûsã al-Yûsufî (d. 1357 C.E.), author of *Kashf-ul-Kurûb fi Ma'rifat-il-Hurûb*; Muhammad bin Manklî (d. 1377 C.E.), author of *al-Tadbîrãt-ul-Sultãnîyah fi Siyãsat-il-Sanã'i'-il-Harbîyah; al-Akhãm-ul-Mulûkîyah w-al-Dawãbit-ul-*

Nãmûsîyah on the art of fighting; and *Uns-ul-Malã bi-Wahsh-il-Falã* on hunting; Muhammad bin Lãjîn al-Rammãh (d. 1379 C.E.), author of *Bughyat-ul-Qãsidîn f-il-'Amal b-il-Mayãdîn* on horsemanship in the battle-field; and Tîbughã al-Ashrafî (d. 1396 C.E.), author of *al-Jihãd w-al-Furûsîyah; Ghunyat-ul-Tullãb fî Ma'rifat-il-Rumh w-al-Nushshãb*, etc.[25]

Conclusion

In the light of the above introductory account it would be no exaggeration to conclude that the achievements made by the scientists and scholars under the Mamluk rule are so outstanding and impressive that no other Islamic dynasty of the later medieval periods can be put on a par with it in this respect. It is indeed surprising to know that the Mamluk rulers, despite their having been rough, illiterate and hot-blooded soldiers, had an appreciably keen interest in the cultivation of knowledge and learning. This also adequately reflects how greatly inspired they might have been by the spirit of Islam to provide a congenial atmosphere for the promotion of study and research in their domain.

Now permit me to close my address with due emphasis on the point that there is a growing need for undertaking serious research works on the scientific and civilizational contributions made by the Arabs and the Persians. As is well-known, thousands of manuscripts on scientific subjects in Arabic and Persian are still lying scattered in different libraries all over the world that are yet to see the light of day. If they are properly edited and published as well as studied and analysed, they are bound not only to throw floodlight of fresh information on the subject, but also give these peoples their rightful place in the history of science and civilization.

Finally, I thank you once again for the patient hearing you have so kindly given to me.

NOTES AND REFERENCES

1. Joseph Hell, *The Arab Civilization* (tr. into English by K. Buksh), p. 117.
2. *Ibid.*, p. 117.
3. *Dã'irat-ul-Ma'ãrif*, Beirut, 1958, Vol. IV, p. 108.
4. Abdul Ali, *Arab-Islamic Legacy to Life Sciences*, Delhi, 1993, pp. 38-43.
5. *The Genius of Arab Civilization*, edited by S.K. Hamarneh, p. 182.
6. P.K. Hitti, *History of the Arabs*, p. 687.
7. *Ibid.*, pp. 685-686.
8. Jurjî Zaydãn, *Tãrîkh Ãdãb-il-Lughat-il-'Arabîyah*, Cairo, Vol. III, p. 270.
9. P.K. Hitti, *op.cit.*, p. 686.
10. See "*Wasful Hiwal 'Inda Ibn-il-Nafîs*" by Nashat al-Hamarneh in the Journal *Tãrîkh-ul-'Ulûm-il-'Arabîyah*, Jamia Halab 1984, Vol. III, Nos. 1 & 2.
11. E.J. Brill, *First Encyclopedia of Islam*, Vol. III, p. 405.
12. *Arab-Islamic Legacy to Life Sciences*, op.cit., p. 86.
13. *The Genius of Arab Civilization*, op.cit., p. 183.
14. P.K. Hitti, *op.cit.*, p. 683.
15. Qadrî Hãfiz Tûqãn, *Turãth-ul-'Arab-il-'Ilmî,* Cairo, 1954, p. 391.
16. *Ibid.*, p. 392.
17. *Ibid.*, p. 388.
18. Jurjî Zaydãn, *op.cit.*, p. 251; Qadrî Hãfiz Tûqãn, *op.cit.*, p. 410.
19. R.A. Nicholson, *A Literary History of the Arabs*, p. 452.

20. Khayruddin al-Ziriklî *Al-A 'lãm*, Beirut, 1980, Vol. VI, p. 156.
21. Ahmad Shalabî, *Mawsû 'at-ul-Tãrîkh-il-Islãmî*, Cairo, 1990, Vol. V, p. 275.
22. R.A. Nicholson, *op.cit.*, p. 453.
23. See "The Arabs as Seafarers" by Abdul Ali in *Islamic Culture*, Vol. LIV, No. 4, 1980, pp. 211-222.
24. P.K. Hitti, *op.cit.*, p. 689.
25. Jurjî Zaydãn, *op.cit.*, pp. 275-277.

PRESIDENTIAL ADDRESS: ISLAMIC STUDIES SECTION,

38th Session, A.I.O.C., Jadavpur (1997)

Fellow Delegates and Learned Scholars,

First, I express my deep sense of gratitude to the Executive Council of the All-India Oriental Conference for giving me the honour to chair the Islamic Studies Section of the Conference for the fourth time. In my previous presidential address presented at the Islamic Studies Section of the 35th Session of the Conference held at Hardwar in 1990, I had discussed in some detail the contributions made by Muslim scientists in the domain of life sciences. I, therefore, propose to assess and analyze in this address the lofty contributions made by Arab-Muslim scientists in the field of exact sciences, particularly mathematics, astronomy and physics. And before proceeding further I would like to submit with all humility that the main reason for taking up the treatment of purely scientific subjects in my address is that the work done by our scholars and institutions is negligible in comparison to the tremendous contributions made by Muslim scientists to the advancement of our scientific knowledge. As such I seek to draw your attention to the need for study and investigation in this fertile but neglected area of research in the discipline of Islamic Studies.

It is a well-known fact that when the fact-finding Arabs established their empire and got access to the legacy of the then civilized world, they first of all paid attention to the practical sciences of immediate advantage and benefit to them and to the whole mankind. It was with this end in view that they took to the cultivation of different branches of science on a priority basis. A brief sketch of their contributions in the exact sciences is attempted below.

Mathematics and Astronomy

As in other sciences, in mathematics and astronomy also the first valuable contribution made by the Muslim Arabs was that they got translated into Arabic the main Greek and Indian works on these subjects. That way they not only drew benefits from the past intellectual legacy of the world, but also preserved it for the future generations. An idea of the importance of these services rendered by them may be had from the fact that a good number of ancient scientific works are available today only in their Arabic translations.

The main Greek works that were translated into Arabic on these subjects were the *Elements* of Euclid (fl. c. 300 BC), the most prominent Greek geometrician; the *Conics* of Apollonius (b. c. 262 BC); the *Spherics* of Menelaus (fl. late 1st century CE) on the geometry of the sphere; the *Almagest* and *Quadripartitum* of Ptolemy (fl. in the 2nd century CE), the distinguished Greek astronomer, geographer and mathematician. The noted translators from the Greek and Syriac languages into Arabic were Abû Yahyã Bin al-Batrîq (d. c̲. 806); al-Hajjãj Bin Yûsuf Bin Matar (fl. between 786 and 833); Hunayn Bin Ishãq (809-73); T̲h̲ãbit Bin Qurrah (d. 901); and Qustã Bin Lûqã (d. c̲. 922), etc.

As regards the important Sanskrit works on mathematics and astronomy that were translated and studied by the Arabs, mention may be made of *Aryabhatiya* by Aryabhatta, the renowned Indian mathematician of the fifth century CE, and *Brahma-Sphuta-Siddhanta* (Ar. *Sindhind*), a treatise on astronomy by Brahmagupta (d. after 665 CE). Other major Indian works translated into Arabic were *al-Arkand* by Brahmagupta;

Kitãb Asrãr al-Mawãlîd by Kanakah; *Kitãb fi 'Ilm al-Nujûm* by Chanakya, etc.

The important astronomical work *Siddhanta* was introduced to the Arabs in Baghdad by the celebrated Indian physician Mankalf in the time of Caliph al-Mansûr in 771. It was translated into Arabic by Muhammad Bin Ibrãhîm al-Fazãrî. It was mainly from this book that the Arabs learned the Indian numeral system and the zero, the invention of which around the second century BC is reckoned as one of the greatest mathematical achievements of all times.[1]

The most significant contribution of the Arabs in arithmetic was that they soon learned, adopted and systematized the Indian decimal system of reckoning which could express any big number by means of only nine figures and the symbol of zero. This sharply contrasted with the cumbersome systems of reckoning adopted by the Greeks and the Romans. As is well-known, the Romans used the seven letters of their alphabet, namely, I,V,X,L,C,D and M for reckoning 1,5,10,50,100, 500 and 1000 respectively.[2] Needless to say that under this handicapped system of reckoning the science of calculation could have never developed into its present sophisticated form of tremendous capacity. But the defect with the Indian figures was that they were not yet unified. And the credit for unifying them into one fixed series of forms goes to the Arabs.[3] When introduced into Europe through the Arabs, these figures became known there as Arabic numerals despite the fact that the Arabs themselves always referred to them in their writings as Indian numerals. Thus armed with the tool of the decimal system of calculation, the Arab-Muslim mathematicians left their indelible impact on all the three remaining branches of mathematics, namely, algebra, geometry and trigonometry.

The Arabs' achievements in algebra were so great that it was rightly called the product of the Arab genius. No wonder, the word 'algebra' itself is of Arabic origin which was first used by Muhammad Bin Mûsã al-Khwarizmî (780-850). The Arabs were also the first to use the algebraic symbols. They solved equations of the first, second, third and fourth degrees. They also succeeded in solving cubic equations by intersecting conics which, in the words of Cajori, "was the greatest achievement of the Arabs in algebra".[4]

In the science of geometry also the Arabs are credited with having laid down the foundations of analytical geometry by using algebraic methods for the solution of geometrical problems and geometrical methods for the solution of algebraic problems. This is despite the fact that the Greeks, whose contribution in arithmetic and algebra was nil, had already so highly developed the science of geometry by laying down its theorems that there was hardly any scope for further development in this field.[5]

Another important contribution of the Arabs in geometry was that they took up study of this science at a time when it had been completely ignored by all other peoples. It was mainly through the Arabs that the Greek legacy to geometry was transmitted to Europe. This is clear from the fact that Latin versions of the works of Arab geometricians were studied as textbooks in Europe until the close of the sixteenth century. It was only after this period that the European scholars stumbled upon Euclid's theorems of geometry in the original Greek language.[6]

Again, in trigonometry the Arab contribution was so overwhelming that this branch of mathematics came to be known as an Arab science. Although this science was known to both the Greeks and the Indians, it was yet in its preliminary form which was mostly studied as a subsidiary branch of astronomy. But the Arabs not only developed it into a separate science independent of astronomy, but also became the founders of both plane and spherical trigonometry which did not exist among the Greeks.[7]

In addition to the above, the Arabs are also credited with having drawn up different tables which ultimately led to the invention of the science of logarithms. It is worthy of mention in this context that while Sinãn al-Hãsib (fl. in the ninth century) was the first Arab mathematician who gave the idea of logarithms, Ibn Yûnûs (d. 1009) composed the first such table for facilitating numerical calculation about 607 years ahead of John Napier who is wrongly credited by Western historians with the invention of logarithms.[8]

Likewise, astronomy was another important exact science to which the Arab-Muslim scientists paid their particular attention. But when they became acquainted with the legacy of astronomy as practiced by the Babylonians, the Greeks and the Chinese, they found that it had degenerated into astrology which aimed at finding out some connection between the movements and positions of the stars and human life. It goes to the credit of the Arabs that they cultivated astronomy as a pure mathematical science devoid of the astrological fancy which remained dominant on the European mind until the seventeenth century.[9] As described by Professor Jardaq, "the Muslim Arabs were the first to reject astrology as valueless and based on fancy; in the study of the stars they favoured truths built upon observation, study and experiment."[10]

The Muslim scientists were interested in astronomy for practical purposes. The need for determining the direction for travellers crossing the desert as well as for knowing the exact times of prayers and the first appearance of the moon gave religious incentive to their study of astronomy and geography. Besides, the following and similar Qur'ãnic Verses are also said to have inspired them to undertake scientific study of astronomy:

> It is He Who made the sun
> To be a shining glory
> And the moon to be a light
> (Of beauty), and measured out
> Stages for her; that ye might
> Know the number of years

And the count (of time).
Nowise did God create this
But in truth and righteousness.
Thus doth He explain His Sings
In detail, for those who understand.[11]
And the Sun
Runs his course
For a period determined
For him: that is
The decree of (Him),
The Exalted in Might,
The All-Knowing.
And the Moon -
We have measured for her
Mansions (to traverse)
Till she returns
Like the old (and withered)
Lower part of a date-stalk.
It is not permitted
To the Sun to catch up
The Moon, nor can
The Night outstrip the Day:
Each (just) swims along
In (its own) orbit
(According to Law).[12]

An idea of the great interest taken by Muslim rulers and scientists in the cultivation of astronomy, the mother of sciences, may be had from the big number of observatories built by them across the Islamic world. The first Shammãsîyah Observatory was built by Caliph al-Mãmûn (ruled 913-33 CE) in Baghdad for the astronomers Fadl Bin al-Nawbakht and Muhammad Bin Mûsã al-Khwãrizmî. It was followed by the establishment of two observatories, one built by al-Battãnî at Raqqah in Syria and the other by 'Abdul Rahmãn al-Sûfi at-Shîrãz.[13] The other prestigious observatories included those at: Hamadan founded by the Persian ruler 'Ala al-Dawlah for Ibn Sînã in 1023; Toledo in Muslim Spain, headed by al-Zarqãlî (d. 1091 CE); Maraghah built by Hulãgû Khãn in 1261 and directed by Nasîr al-Dîn al-Tûsî; Samarkand, founded by Ulugh Beg, a distinguished astronomer, in the 15th century; and Istanbul, founded by the Ottoman Sultan, Murãd III, and directed by his court astronomer Taqî al-Dîn in the 16th century.

The scientific data collected at those observatories greatly improved understanding of the planetary motions, as a result of which the Muslim astronomers achieved striking results which laid down the foundation of modern astronomy. The astronomical tables prepared by them containing information on dates, prayer times, the azimuth of Makkah and related matters represented a unique Islamic contribution to the development of mathematical astronomy.[14] Among numerous other achievements, they established that the earth is a sphere floating in space, that the earth is smaller than the sun, and that the moon varies its orbit from year to year. They also accurately measured the circumference of the earth as well as "calculated the length of the stellar year as 365 days, six hours, nine minutes and ten seconds, which is only half a second more than the actual length of the year."[15]

The Muslim scientists are also credited with having improved and invented several minute astronomical instruments and appliances for studying the planets and the stars as well as for measuring their distance from the earth and from one another. The great lasting impact left by them on this science may be guaged from the fact that about half of the stars that are known to us still carry Arabic names.[16] As rightly described by Paul Lunde, "the influence of these astronomical works was immense. Today, for example, the very appellations of the constellations still bear the names given them by Muslim astronomers - Acrob (from '*aqrab*, 'scorpion'), Altair (from *al-tãir*, the 'flyer'), Deneb (from *dhanb*, 'tail'), Pherkard (from *farqad*, 'calf') - and words such as zenith, nadir and azimuth, all still in use today, recalls the works of the Muslim scholars....."[17]

Eminent Muslim Mathematicians and Astronomers

The Muslim world produced a large number of mathematicians and astronomers. About 1,087 books on these subjects were written in Arabic alone between the eight and fifteenth centuries of the Christian era, out of which 1,043 books, 96% of the total output, were authored by Muslim scientists.[18] If the books produced by them in the other Oriental languages, especially Persian and Turkish, are also counted, the number would definitely become much greater than this. Here it is not possible within the limits of this address to give a comprehensive account of their contributions in these sciences. But the names of al-Khwãrizmî, al-Battãnî, 'Alî Bin Yûnus, al-Bîrûnî and Nasîr al-Dîn al-Tûsî, to mention only a few, are very famous for cultivation of the mathematical sciences in Islam. Their achievements are briefly mentioned below.

Muhammad Bin Mûsã al-Khwãrizmî

Muhammad Bin Mûsã al-Khwãrizmî (780-850 CE), the greatest mathematical genius of Islam, flourished in the time of Caliph al-Mãmûn. He was the first and the most eminent author on arithmetic and algebra. Unfortunately, the original Arabic versions of both books are lost. They are extant today only in their Latin translations. His *Hisãb al-Jabr w-al-Muqãbalah* (The Calculation of Integration and Equation) was translated into Latin by Gerard of Cremona in the twelfth century, while the Latin version of his book on arithmetic was edited and published by Prince Boncompagni at Rome in 1857 under the title *De Numero Indico*.

Both these works served as the principal text-books of European universities for several centuries. It was mainly through these books that the Indian numerals called algorithms after the author were introduced into the West which soon brought about a revolution in the science of calculation. It is in recognition of his contributions as mathematician that the first half of the ninth century is characterized by G. Sarton as the time of al-Khwãrizmî.[19]

Al-Battãnî

Abû 'Abdullãh Muhammad Bin Jãbir al-Battãnî (850-925) was one of greatest Muslim mathematicians and astromers of all times. He rectified Ptolemy's astronomical calculations for the orbits of certain planets by replacing geometrical methods with trigonometry. He also pointed out that the position of the sun's apogee, or farthest point from the earth, is variable. He made astronomical observations of remarkable accuracy relating to the obliquity of the ecliptic, annual eclipses of the sun and the determination of the visibility of the new moon.[20] In addition, he accurately computed sine, tangent, and contangent tables from zero to 90 degrees.[21] Several books on mathematics and astronomy are attributed to him. But his claim to fame rests on his *Handbook of Astronomical Tables* which remained influential in the West until the Renaissance.[22] This book was translated into Latin in 1116 and into Spanish in the thirteenth century.[23] It is said to have exercised a deep influence on the development of astronomy and spherical trigonometry in medieval Europe.[24]

'Alî Bin Yûnus

Abul Hasan 'Alî Bin Yûnus (d. 1009) was put in charge of the Muqattam Observatory. His principal work is titled as *al-Zîj al-Hãkimî* (The Hãkimî Astronomical Tables) after his patron Caliph al-Hãkim, in which he improved the tables of his predecessors by original observations. It is unfortunate that his tables could not be completely preserved. Only some protions of the tables are now available in Leiden, Oxford, Paris, the Escorial, Berlin and Cairo.[25]

Ibn Yûnus is also credited with the invention of the pendulum for measuring time about six centuries ahead of Galileo, who on his turn studied the subject thoroughly and laid down most of the laws regarding it and its arithmetical implications. It is rightly believed by scientists that but for this the astronomical science could never have advanced to the position it holds today.[26]

Al-Bîrûnî

Abû Rayhãn Muhammad Bin 'Ahmad al-Bîrûnî (973-1050), renowned as the Ptolemy of his age, was a remarkable genius of his time and one of the greatest intellectual minds of all times. He was a distinguished astronomer, mathematician, geographer and physicist. He contributed a great deal to the development of mathematical geography. He calculated the circumference of the earth as 24,779 miles which is less than the actual measurement only by 78 miles. The geographical model of the world and of mankind given by him is accurate to an appreciable extent. He has described the habitable region of the world as follows:

> "The plane of the equinoctical cuts the earth at a circle called the equator (*Khatt al-Istiwã*) into two parts, northern and southern hemispheres. A great circle drawn through the poles divides these two into four quadrants, two northern and two southern. Those who have investigated the matter find that the dry land does not extend beyond one of the northern quadrants. This is, therefore, called the habitable quadrant. It is as if it were an island surrounded by the sea. In this quarter which men are constantly traversing, they find seas,

> islands, mountains, rivers and deserts, also towns and villages until towards the north pole a desolate tract is reached of excessive cold, where snows are heaped on snows".[27]

In addition to the above, al-Bîrûnî made a series of observations on solar transits, lunar eclipses, equinoxes and solstices. He also scientifically described such phenomena as the ebb and flow of tides, earthquakes, petrified remains of living creatures and even continental shifts.[28] Besides, he propounded his theory of the rotation of the earth on its axis about 600 years ahead of Galileo (1564-1642 CE). This is clear from the following passage from his *Canon Masudicus*:

"When a thing falls from a height, it does not coincide with the perpendicular line of its descent, but inclines a little, and falls making different angles. When a piece of earth separates from it and falls, it has two kinds of motion: one is the circular motion which it receives from the rotation of the earth, and the other is straight which it acquires in falling directly to the centre of the earth. If it had only the straight motion, it would have fallen to the west of its perpendicular motion. But since both of them exist at one and the same time, it falls neither to the west nor in the perpendicular direction, but a little to the east."[29]

Nasîr al-Dîn al-Tûsî

Nasîr al-Dîn al-Tûsî (1201-1274) made substantial progress in trigonometry and planetary astronomy. It was mainly because of his efforts that trigonometry achieved the status of an independent branch of pure mathematics. His most original book on this subject is *Kitãb Shakl al-Qattã'*, a work on the principle of the transversal, from which he deduced relations of fundamental importance in spherical trigonometry.[30] It was translated into Latin, French and English, upon which the Europeans depended for a long time for their knowledge of plane and spherical trigonometry. For instance, it was upon the same book that Regiomontanus largely depended in the preparation of his own work on trigonometry under the titled *De Triangulus*.[31]

Another major contribution of al-Tûsî was that he and his colleagues at the Maraghah Observatory succeeded in getting the close value of precession as 51" (actually 50.26").[32] Further, he considerably advanced the knowledge of planetary astronomy by producing better planetary models which had a great similarity with those of the Polish astronomer, Nicolaus Copernicus. In it he has critised Ptolemy for his views expressed in the *Almagest*. It was this criticism which enabled Copernicus to enunciate his theory of the celestial bodies which had far-reaching implications for the rise of modern science.[33]

Physics

Although a great deal of literature produced by Muslim scientists in the field of physics and allied subjects is lost to posterity, yet the extant literature is sufficient enought to give us a clear idea of the progress made by them in this branch of scientific knowledge. They achieved distinctions in finding out the specific gravity of different substances as well as in optics and the atmospheric transmission of light. Abû Yûsuf Ya'qûb Bin Ishãq al-Kindî (d. 873 CE), Ibn Sînã (d. 1037 CE), Ibn al-Haytham (d. 1039 CE), al-Bîrûnî (d. 1050 CE), Abû al-Fath 'Abdul Rahmãn al-Mansûr al-Khãzinî (fl. early 12th century), Qutb al-Dîn al-Shîrãzî (d. 1311 CE) and Kamãl al-Dîn al-Fãrisî (d. about 1320 CE), to mention only a few, were eminent Muslim physicists, who contributed a great deal to the development of this science. Of them Ibn al-Haytham was the most prominent, who is regarded as one of the greatest physicists of all times in recognition of his spectacular contribution to optics. His achievements are briefly mentioned below.

Ibn al-Haytham

Al-Hasan Ibn al-Haytham (965-1039), popularly known in the West as Alhazen, never lived a settled life. He travelled from place to place meeting scholars and making observations on natural phenomena. About a hundred works on different subjects, especially mathematics, astronomy, optics, philosophy and medicine, are ascribed to him. But his claim to fame rests on his *Kitãb al-Manãzir* (The Book of Optics) which is described by Will Durant as probably the most thoroughly scientific work in its method and thought of all the medieval writings.[34]

Ibn al-Haytham's glaring achievement in the field of optics was that he repudiated the prevalent Greek theory of vision, and presented a correct theory of the process of visual perception, according to which vision occurs when light emanating from the seen object enters the eye rather than when a ray of light sent by the eye reaches the object as held by Euclid and Ptolemy. He made several other important observations on light which had far-reaching implications in the world of science. For example, prior to his research, the prevalent view was that light does not take time in reaching from one place to another. It was he who first propounded the theory that light travels at a tremendous but fixed speed. But this idea was severely criticised in the West unuil Romer hinted at its possibility towards the end of the seventeenth century after observing two lunar eclipses.[35] Besides, he anticipated Fermat's principle of Least Time by several centuries by pointing out that a ray of light takes the easier and quicker path in passing through a medium. He also discovered the law of inertia which became the forerunner of Newton's first law of motion.[36]

Ibn al-Haytham also discovered in his *On Twilight Phenomena*, which is now extant only in Latin, the effect of refraction and reflection of light in increasing the apparent size of the sun or the moon near the horizon at the time of their rising or setting, and concluded that through atmospheric refraction the light of the sun reaches the earth even when the sun is as much as 19 degrees below the horizon. On this basis he calculated the height of the atmospheric layer as about 10 English miles.[37] His research on the reflection and refraction of light is said to have become the precursor of the camera.

These and other theories laid down by Ibn al-Haytham had a great impact on the advancement of science in the West. This should be clear from the fact that now it is established beyond doubt that such eminent European scientists as Roger Bacon, Witelo, Kepler, Leonardo, etc., were greatly influenced by his researches.[38]

Conclusion

It is sufficiently clear from the above brief introduction to the contributions made by the Arab-Muslim scientists in the field of the exact sciences that they religiously cultivated scientific knowledge as well as shared it with their non-Muslim brethren for the sole constructive purpose of improving the lot of the whole mankind. And in the process they became harbingers of the modern scientific era by handing over to the West what they had acquired and learned from the ancients in its highly enriched form embodying their own valuable additions. This is despite the fact that large numbers of valuable manuscripts produced by them have already perished.

But it is a matter of regret that although a vast body of literature is still extant on these and other natural sciences, the contents and details of most of the scientific works are lying buried in the manuscripts that are preserved in libraries scattered in different parts of the world, especially in those of Europe, America and the Muslim world. I would further like to point out in this context that a good number of manuscripts were produced by Indian Muslim scientists also during the Sultanate and Mughal periods in different sciences, particularly mathematics, astronomy, time-measuring devices, music and medicine. Their legacy also has not yet received the attention of our scholars it deserves.

In view of the facts mentioned above, I would like to stress the need for research into the unexplored works of Muslim scientists, for what has been done so far is only a small fraction of the vast available literature. It is, therefore, highly desirable that we should study and edit the manuscripts by the application of the critical and comparative method. Needless to say that this task can be greatly facilitated if subject-wise descriptive catalogues are prepared and made available to the researchers. Likewise, while the need for procuring microfilm copies of rare manuscripts cannot be overemphasized, they may also be sought to be put into the Internet system with a view to enabling the scholars to make full use of these otherwise hardly accessible treasures. It is also equally important that we should undertake a co-ordinated programme for translating major Arabic and Persian works on scientific subjects into other languages, particularly English, Urdu and Hindi, for the benefit of the historians of science not acquainted with these source languages. But these objectives cannot be realized except by sustained and co-ordinated efforts of teams of devoted scholars.

Learned scholars and fellow delegates, I have taken much of your valuable time. Before I close my address, I thank you once again for the patient hearing you have so kindly given to me.

NOTES AND REFERENCES

1. P.K. Hitti, *History of the Arabs*, London, 1958, pp. 378-379.
2. 'Abdul Rahmãn al-Badawî, *Dawr al-'Arab fi Takwîn al-Fikr al-'Ilmî al-Awrubbî*, Cairo, 1967, p. 17.
3. Cajori, *A History of Mathematics*, p. 100.
4. *Ibid.*, p. 107.
5. Omar A. Farrukh, *The Arab Genius is Sceicne and Philosòphy,* Washington, 1954, p. 40.
6. *Ibid.*, p. 40.
7. *Ibid.*, p. 42.
8. *Ibid.*, p. 42.
9. *Ibid.*, p. 43
10. *Ibid.*, p. 43.
11. The Qur'ãn, X:5-6 (tr. by A. Yusuf Ali).
12. The Qur'ãn, XXXVI:38-40 (tr. by A. Yusuf Ali).
13. C.A. Qadir, *Philosophy and Science in the Islamic World*, New York, 1988, p. 116.
14. Mohammad Ilyãs: "Islamic Develoment of Astronomy: Role of Religious Practices and State Patronage" in *Hamdard Islamicus*, Pakistan, Vol. XVII, No. 3, 1994, p. 23.
15. Omar A. Farrukh, *op.cit.*, pp. 44-45.
16. *Ibid.*, p.. 45.
17. Paul Lunde, *Science: The Islamic Legacy*, pp. 22-23; quoted by C.A. Qadir, *op.cit.*, pp. 116-117.
18. Mohammad Ilyãs, *op.cit.*, p. 31.
19. 'Alî Abdullãh al-Daffa', *The Muslim Contribution to Mathematics*, London, 1977, p. 50.

20. P.K. Hitti, *op.ict.*, p. 370.
21. 'Alî Abdullãh al-Daffa', *op.cit.*, p. 71.
22. *Ibid.*, p. 70.
23. *The New Encyclopaedia Britannica*, Vol. I, 15th Edition, Chicago, 1994, p. 962.
24. 'Alî 'Abdullãh al-Daffa', *op.cit.*, p. 72.
25. E.J. Brill, *First Encyclopaedia of Islam*, Vol. III, pp. 428-429.
26. Omar A. Farrukh, *op.cit.*, pp. 67-68.
27. Ibrahim Boolaky: "The Mathmatical Geography of al-Bîrûnî" in *Hamdard Islamicus*, Pakistan, Vol. VII, No. 2, 1984, pp. 64-65.
28. *Ibid.*, p. 66.
29. M.M. Sharif, edited *A History of Muslim Philosophy*, 1966, Vol. II, p. 1229.
30. E.J. Brill, *First Encyclopaedia of Islam*, Vol. VIII, p. 981.
31. Qadrî Hãfiz Tûqãn, *Al-'Ulûm 'ind-al-'Arab*, p. 210.
32. Sayyed Hossein Nasr in *Dictionary of Scientific Biography*, New York, Vol. XIII, p. 509.
33. Dr. 'Abdul 'Azîm Anîs: "Nasîr al-Dîn al-Tûsî" in the Journal *al-'Arabî*, Kuwait, No. 330 (May 1986), pp. 37-39.
34. Will Durent, *The Story of Civilization*, Vol. IV, p. 288.
35. N. Shahin: "Hasan Bin al-Haytham" in *Qãfilah al-Zayt* (August 1976), Saudi Arabia, p. 38.
36. Professor Abdus Salam: "Islam and Science" in *Hamdard Medicus*, Pakistan, Vol. XXIX, No. 4, p. 5.
37. Will Durant, *op.cit.*, p. 288.
38. *Ibid.*, p. 289.

PRESIDENTIAL ADDRESS: ISLAMIC STUDIES SECTION,

39th Session, A.I.O.C., Vadodara (1998)

Distinguished Delegates and Scholars,

I am deeply grateful to the authorities of the All-India Oriental Conference for considering me worthy of the honour they have done me by electing me to preside over the deliberations of the Islamic Studies Section of the 39th Session of the Conference. At the outset I would like to point out that my previous two presidential addresses were devoted to the discussion of the need for research into the contributions made by Arab-Muslim scientists to the growth and development of life and exact sciences in the West. I, therefore, crave your indulgence and seek your permission to deal in this address with some of the remaining important aspects of the transmission of varied Arabico-Persian and Islamic elements into the cultural heritage of Europe with particular reference to the role played by Arab-Islamic literary genres in the development of modern European literature, especially fiction literature including fables, short stories, novels and dramas.

It is a well-known fact of history that there had been four main channels of transmission of Arab-Islamic thoughts and ideas into the West which took place through both oral traditions and writings. First, there existed a hectic commercial exchange across the Mediterranean Sea between its northern European littoral states and its southern Arab littoral states. It is said that through the merchants and traders a lot of information about Arab-Islamic culture and literature early reached as far in northern Europe as Scandinavia.

Secondly, the Crusaders who conquered and ruled several states in Muslim Asia, particularly Syria and Palestine, also played an important role in the cultural and intellectual interaction between the Arabs and the Europeans. The war captives in particular taken by both sides contributed a great deal to the diffusion of the Arab-Islamic cultural and literary heritage in the West.

Thirdly, Muslim rule in Spain and Sicily was the most important channel of the transmission. The visit by Pope Silvester II to Cordova (970-976 C.E.) marked the beginning of the cultural exchange between Muslim Spain and Christian Europe in the time of Caliph al-Hakam II (961-76 C.E.). And the process of transmission of the treasures of Arab-Islamic learning into the West reached its meridian in Toledo following its conquest by the Christians in 1085. There lived in it side by side three important communities the Muslims, the Christians and the Jews, of whom the Jews acted as the main intermediary between the remaining two communities in both trade and translation of Arabic books into Latin. Thanks to the efforts made by Archbishop Raymond I (1126-1152 C.E.), there took place a great translation movement which lasted for more than a century from 1135 to 1284. The method of translation followed was that the Arabic books were first orally translated by Arabicized Jews into Hebrew or the local Spanish dialect before their rendition into Latin.[1]

Lastly, in later times, the domination of the Ottoman Turks in several European countries also led to the introduction and diffusion of several elements of Islamic cultural and literary heritage in the West.

One direct impact of the diffusion of Arabic learning in Europe was that it led to the growth and development of modern European languages to the utter neglect of their own classical languages, Latin and Greek. The Christians of Spain and Sicily soon became thoroughly Arabicized as well as conversant with

Arabic language and literature. Several Spanish, Italian, French and English writers who contributed to the growth and development of Western literature drew heavily on Arabic literature, especially Arabic fiction literature, Arabic models of expression and proverbs. Alvaro, a Spanish Christian writer of Cordova, expressed this phenomenon, saying that his Christian co-religionists had become so much intoxicated with the eloquence and ideas of Arabic language and literature that they read only the poetry and romances of the Arabs, and that they studied only the writings of Muslim theologians and philosophers. He further lamented that the Christian youth studied the Arabic language so thoroughly that they started speaking and writing Arabic like the Arabs, and that they amassed a large library of Arabic books at an enormous cost. They also openly avowed that Arabic language and literature deserved all praise and applause.[2]

The influence of Arab-Islamic literature on European literatures right from the thirteenth century to modern times has been so dominant and pervasive that there lies a fertile field for studies and research in this particular branch of Islamic studies. The main Arabic works that became the forerunner of modern Western literature were the *Kalîlah wa Dimnah,* the *Maqãmãt* of Badî' al-Zamãn and al-Harîrî, *Risãlat al-Ghufrãn* by Abul 'Alã al-Ma'arrî, *the Arabian Nights* etc. A brief introduction of the impact of these Arabic literary genres on European literatures with special reference to *the Arabian Nights* is attempted below with a view to giving you an idea of the role played by Arab-Islamic literature in revolutionizing the European literary thoughts and genres during both the Renaissance period and modern times.

Kalîfah wa Dimnah:

As is well-known, the book *Kalîlah wa Dimnah*, being a collection of fables put into the mouths of animals and birds, is an old Indian Sanskrit work which was translated into Pahlawi

(Middle Persian) by order of the Sassanid king Khusraw Anushirwan (531-579 C.E.). This book was intended to guide people to right behaviour as well as to instruct rulers in the laws of polity, It also contains a fine analytical account of human sentiments and human weaknesses. It was translated into Arabic by Ibn al-Muqaffa' in the middle of the eighth century C.E. This Arabic version became not only one of the earliest prose-works in Arabic, but also the basis of all existing translations into the major languages of the world.

The Arabic version of the book was first translated into Spanish in 1251 which subsequently became the first attempt at story-writing in this European language.[3] Then it was translated into Hebrew, Latin and other European languages, following which the stories contained in it not only became popular in Europe, but also exercised a major influence on the development of prose and story-writing in the West as it was heavily drawn upon by several European writers in their respective works in Latin and other languages.[4]

The overwhelming impact of the book *Kalîlah wa Dimnah* is clearly visible in a number early collections of Latin stories. An illustrious example of this fact is the Latin book *Disciplina Clericalis* compiled by Butrus Alfonso (fl. in the 12th century C.E.), who translated and incorporated in it at least one-third of the stories from different Arabic sources.[5] Another glaring instance of the impact of the book on story-writing in the West is the collection of Latin stories compiled by an unknown writer under the title *Geste Romanorum*. It has been found out by researchers that most of the stories and fables contained in it are taken from *Kalîlah wa Dimnah* and other Arabic sources.[6]

Further, the renowned French writer Gean de La Fontaine (1621-1695 C.E.) clearly admitted to having been greatly influenced by the beast stories of *Kalîlah wa Dimnah*. It is quite obvious that he took he basic material of his *Fables*, ranking among the greatest masterpieces of French literature, from this great Arabic work of Indian origin and other Eastern sources.[7]

The Maqãmãt:

The *Maqãmah*-writing originated by Badî' al-Zamãn al-Hamadhãnî (969-1008 C.E.) and perfected by al-Harîrî (1054-1122 C.E.) marked the culmination of the development of rimed prose and flowery diction in classical Arabic. Written in the form of dramatic anecdotes, the *Maqãmãt* became the most elaborate of all Arabic compositions. The *Maqãmãt* of al-Harîrî are still studied in all centres of Arabic studies across the globe as, next to the Holy Qur'ãn, the chief treasure of the literary Arabic tongue. They also came closer to the Western concept of short story. Far from being mere frivolous stories, the anecdotes described in them in a dramatic manner are also aimed at criticising the existing social order as well as drawing moral lessons from them.[8]

The impact of these *Maqãmãt* is clearly discernible in the development of rimed prose of Western literature. The affinities and similarities that exist between the episodes of the *Maqãmãt* and the early Spanish and Italian tales deserve to be further studied and explored. Besides, the essays written by such writers as Addison and Steele also bear indelible marks of the influence of these *Maqãmãt*.[9]

The Arabian Nights:

Like their cultivation of other sciences, the Arabs did not lag behind in the field of narrating tales and fables also. Although they paid attention to the development of fiction literature at a later stage during the decadent phase of their history, they left their indelible marks in this field also. Initially, they borrowed the art of narrating tales from the Persians who had produced such famous works on this subject as *Hazãr Afsãnã* and *Gulistãn-e-Sadi*. When these works were translated into Arabic, they soon became very popular among the Arab masses. Their immediate appeal tempted Arab story-tellers to produce similar stories on the pattern of the Persian tales. They practised the art of inventing and narrating tales so successfully that they soon surpassed even the Persians, from whom they had learnt it. They also gave to the world a unique collection of stories known as *The Thousand and One Nights* which is regarded as one of the immortal pieces of international literature.[10]

Its Popularity and Impact

It is interesting to note that the book which remained neglected in its homeland, found recognition in Europe as a valuable ethnographical work. That was the main reason why the Europeans paid special attention to it, thoroughly studied and translated it into their languages. It was mainly because of the great interest taken by them, both intellectuals and masses, in this work that it assumed its place among the most important pieces of international literature.

Obviously, the main cause of success of *The Arabian Nights* in the West was the crisis through which European literature was passing owing to the unprecedented expansion of the reading classes, who demanded a more popular type of literature. As is well-known, in the wake of the expansion of Islam the infiltration of Islamic ideas and of Arabic literary themes into medieval Europe made the Europeans fed up with the monotonous, narrow ecclesiastical disciplines of the Dark Ages. As a direct result of this phenomenon, the European writers started feeling their way towards a new style. And *The Arabian Nights* provided them with the model and clue, for which they were searching, for it possessed the two basic qualities, the spirit of adventure and the element of realism, that are indispensable in a popular literature.[11]

It is remarkable to note that while the tales are the products of the creative imagination of the Arabs, an element of realism is always present in them. Thus these wondrous stories, while providing fantastic entertainment to the readers, not only reflect to a great extent the temperament of the Arab people, but also exude an unfailing, deep wisdom of life acquired through the ages. For instance, the folk-manners and customs were drawn from the society as the narrators saw around them. Similarly, the adventures of Sindbãd, the sailor, which form one of the best known tales of *The Arabian Nights*, have been recognised as based on actual reports of voyages made by Muslim merchants.[12]

Although *The Arabian Nights* in its present form reached Europe in the seventeenth century, some of the stories were narrated in Italy and Spain as early as the thirteenth century. No wonder, the noted Italian writer Giovanni Boccaccio (1313-1375 C.E.) derived the Oriental tales incorporated in the masterpiece *Decameron* from oral traditions.[13] *The Arabian Nights* soon fired the imagination of the Western people, due to which it was in great demand everywhere. An idea of the popularity of the book in the West may be drawn from the fact that it was published in England and France more than thirty times in the eighteenth century, as a result of which some of its stories and characters became an inseparable part of Western folk-lore. It was soon translated into French and English as well as into all the major languages of Europe, namely Dutch, German, Italian, Spanish, Swedish, Russian, Polish, etc.

In view of the overwhelming impact *The Arabian Nights* has exerted on European literature, it would be no exaggeration to say that but for it there would have been no literary renaissance in the West in the field of fiction literature. Contrary to their practice of disowning the Arab-Muslim contributions in other branches of knowledge and learning, especially natural sciences, even the European historians of literature concede that had there not been

The Arabian Nights, there would have been no *Robinson Crusoe*, and no *Gulliver's Travels.*[14]

It is now no longer disputed that almost all the major European writers studied *The Arabian Nights* and were immensely influenced by it. For example, the nenowned French author Voltaire (1694-1778 C.E.) is reported to have said that he had gone through this book as many as fourteen times before he started writing his own stories and novels. Christoph Martin Wieland (1773-1813 C.E.), a renowned German epic poet and man of letters, was another noted European author who borrowed his ideas for his epics from *The Arabian Nights.* He also contributed a great deal to the widening of the German imagination by writing his novels on the basis of psychological development of characters.[15] Similarly, it is held that George Meredith (1828-1909 C.E.), a famous English Victorian poet and novelist, was deeply influenced by *The Arabian Nights* in producing his novels that are noted for their wit, brilliant dialogues and psychological analysis of the characters.[16]

Likewise, the works of William Shakespeare; the *Fairy Tales* of the Grimm brothers of Germany; *Wuthering Heights* by Emily Bronte; *Canterbury Tales* by Geoffrey Chaucer as well as the works of Byron, Wordsworth, Tennyson, Dickens, etc., bear indelible marks of the style and contents of *The Arabian Nights*. Although here it is not possible to give a comprehensive survey of the varied glaring instances of the great impact exerted by the stories of this book on the development of different genres of European fiction literature in the post-Renaissance period, nevertheless a brief reference to the works of Shakespeare and the Grimm brothers is given below for a better appreciation of the infiltration of Arabic style, manners and contents into the European literature.

William Shakespeare

The various elements of Arabism have been found to be so dominant upon the personality and works of William Shakespeare (d. 1616 C.E.) that he appears to have been a product of Arab-Islamic culture and civilization. As rightly described by Prof. Safã Khalûsî of Baghdad, it appears as if a pure Arabian soul had transmigrated into his body. It cannot be a mere coincidence that he has repeatedly mentioned in his works such Arab countries, cities and rivers as Egypt, Syria, Iraq, Tripoli, Halab, Damascus, Jerusalem, Alexandria, the Nile and the Euphrates.[17]

Perhaps, it would be no exaggeration to say that Shakespeare would not have been able to produce his vast literature, especially his five principal plays - Hamlet, Othello, King Lear, Macbeth and Tempest -, had he not drunk deep at the fountains of the rich Arabian sources of knowledge and learning including *The Arabian Nights*. For instance, the vivid, terryfying description of hell given by him in his *Hamlet* has a striking similarity with that in the Qur'ãnic Verses, while his drama *Tempest* resembles the story of the Island of Treasures in *The Arabian Nights*. Both sources are full of description of magicians and devils working under the command of the sultan of the island.[18]

There also exists manifold similarities in matters of both plot and contents between Shakespeare's *Othello* and the story of Qamar al-Zamãn and his beloved in *The Arabian Nights*. The end of the story in both sources is more or less exactly the same. The heroes in both works strangle to death their respective wives on the suspicion of betrayal of trust. The only difference is that while the hero in *The Arabian Nights* named 'Ubaydullãh al-Jawharî is represented more pitiless than Othello, because the former kills not only his wife, but also the slave-girl who used to assist his wife in her misdeeds, Othello is content with killing only his wife. Another point of difference is that while the wife of al-

Jawharî was actually disloyal, Othello's wife Desdemona, with whom he had been in deep love, was innocent. And when Othello himself realised this fact, he resolved upon committing suicide to atone for the sin committed by him.[19]

Shakespeare's other plays, especially *King Lear* and *Merchant of Venice*, also commit to the memory of readers identical contents in *The Arabian Nights*. It is also remarkable to note that those found guilty of ungratefulness and betrayal of trust have been awarded the harshest punishments in both sources.

The Grimm Brothers

The world-famous collection of fairy tales jointly produced by the German philologist Jacob Grimm (1785-1863 C.E.) and his brother Wilhelm Grimm (1786-1859 C.E.) under the title of *Kinder und Hausmarchen,* popularly known as *Grimms' Fairy Tales*, also bear deep marks of *The Arabian Nights* not only on their contents, but also in their style of presentation. The fables were tanscribed by them from oral renderings by the masses. It soon became very popular among the people, as a result of which it was translated into several European languages. And even these days they are prescribed as nursery stories in the West.[20]

The authors themselves have acknowledged in their comments on this book that they have drawn heavily on the stories of *The Arabian Nights*. For example, the story No. 142 titled the *Samlî Mountain* is taken from *The Arabian Nights*' story *'Alî Bãbã and Forty Thieves*. In the German version it is related that when a poor man heard the thieves command mountain Simsî to open, the mountain containing rich treasures opened. Then after packing up rich treasures from it, they got it closed by saying: "O mountain Simsî! Get closed" The poor man also became very rich by using the same sentences. The poor man had an envious brother, who also came to know the trick. But when he entered the mountain, he forgot the sentence by means of which the thieves used to get out of it, because instead of calling 'Simsî', he started calling 'Simlî', 'Simlî'. In the meantime, the thieves entered the mountain and killed him. Obviously, the word 'Simsî' used here is nothing other than the Arabic word 'Simsim' used in *The Arabian Nights*.

Thus *The Arabian Nights* greatly stirred and fired the imagination of Western writers. It not only became an inseparable part of European folklore, but also contributed a great deal to the development of modern literary genres in the West. In view of the great impact this book has exerted on European writers, Professor Massignon has rightly observed that it quickened the mentality of Europe which the Greek and Roman fables had made dull and languid.

In addition to the above, there are several other Arabic works that have left their deep impact on the development of European literature. For instance, Dante (fl. in the 13th century), the pride of Italy, could not have produced his masterpiece *The Divine Comedy,* had he not been acquainted with the contents of such Arabic works as *Risãlat al-Ghufrãn* (treatise on forgiveness) by Abul 'Alã al-Ma'arrî, *al-Futûhãt al-Makkîyah* (the Makkan revelations) by Ibn 'Arabî, and some Arabic texts dealing with the Nocturnal Journey of the Prophet Muhammad (peace be upon him).[22] Besides, the most original contribution of the Spanish Muslim philosopher Ibn Tufayl under the title *Hayy ibn Yaqzãn* (the living one, son of the vigilant) also left a deep religious, philosophical and educational impact on the evolution of European literature. Following its translation into Hebrew in the 14th century and into Latin towards the close of the 17th century, it is claimed to have exercised a great influence over Daniel Defoe in his *Robinson Crusoe* which appeared in 1719.

Lastly, I would like to point out that the impact of the rich Islamic heritage is not confined to the scientific, philosophical and literary advancement of the Europeans. But there lies a big scope for further studies and research on the diffusion of innumerable Islamic elements into several other manifestations of their cultural life such as architecture, fine arts, industries, sanitation, cousine, poetical compositions, music, etc.

Friends, now permit me to close my address with due stress on the need to undertake comprehensive, comparative research works in these and similar unexplored areas of Arabico-Persian and Islamic studies. This will not only authenticate the history of human civilization, but also make possible a true assessment of the role played by Islam and Muslims in enriching human thought and progress in different fields of cultural and civilizational activities.

Finally, I thank you once again for giving me a patient hearing.

NOTES AND REFERENCES

1. 'Abd al-Rahmãn Badawî, *Dawr al-'Arab fi Takwîn al-Firk al-Awrubbî*, Second Edition, Cairo, 1967, pp. 6-8.
2. Ahmad Ibrãhîm al-Sharîf, *Dirãsãt f-il-Hadãrah al-Islãmiyah*, Cairo, 1976, pp. 310-11; Joseph Hell, *The Arab Civilization*, tr. from the German language by S. Khuda Bakhsh, Delhi, Reprint, 1980, p. 103.
3. *The Legacy of Islam*, edited by Thomas Arnold and Alfred Guillaume, Oxford, 1931, p. 30.
4. *Ibid.*, p. 196.
5. *Dawr al-'Arab fi Takwîn al-Fikr al-Awrubbî, op.cit.*, p. 67.
6. *Ibid.*, p. 69.
7. *Dirãsãt f-il-Hadãrah al-Islãmîyah, op.cit.*, p. 311.
8. P.K. Hitti, *History of the Arabs*, London, 1958, p. 403.
9. Ziãuddîn Ahmad, *Influence of Islam on World Civilization*, Delhi, p. 87.
10. Ahmad Hasan al-Zayyãt, *Tãrikh al-Adab al-'Arabî*, Egypt, 1930, p. 340.
11. *The Legacy of Islam, op.cit.*, pp. 197-201.
12. *History of the Arabs, op.cit.*, p. 305.
13. *Ibid.*, p. 613.
14. *The Legacy of Islam, op.cit.*, p. 201.
15. *Dawr al-'Arab fi Takwîn al-Fikr al-Awrubbî, op.cit.*, pp. 101-102; *The New Encyclopaedia Britannica*, 15th edition, 1994, Vol. XII, p. 648.
16. *The New Encyclopaedia Britannica*, Vol. VIII, p. 32.
17. Dr. Safã Khalûsî: "*Shakespeare - Malãmih 'Arabîyah fi Sûratihî wa Adabih*" in the Journal *al-'Arabî*, Kuwait,

No. 56, pp. 58-60.

18. *Ibid.,* p. 60.
19. *Ibid.,* p. 60. See the story of Qamar al-Zamãn and his beloved in *Arabian Nights,* tr. by Sir R.F. Burton, Centenary Edition, London, 1985.
20. *Dawr al-'Arab fi Takwîn al-Fikr al-Awrubbî, op.cit.*, pp. 81-82.
21. *Ibid.,* p. 82.
22. For details, see *Dawr al-'Arab fi Takwîn al-Fikr al-Awrubbî, op.cit.*, pp. 49-65.

PRESIDENTIAL ADDRESS: SOUTH-EAST ASIAN STUDIES SECTION,
40th Session, A.I.O.C., Chennai (2000)

Distinguished Delegates and Friends,

I am deeply grateful to the authorities of the All-India Oriental Conference for the honours shown to me in inviting me to preside over the South-East Asian Studies Section of the 40th Session of the Conference.

The vast South-East Asian region comprising the eastern Asiatic mainland and the immense archipelago including Indonesia and the Philippines, stretches about 4000 miles (6400 kms.) at its farthest extent and covers an area of about 5000,000 square miles. It has been a vital and fertile region for the intermingling and interaction of different historical factors and cultural currents from very ancient times. Its main underlying characteristic is that it is the most diverse region on earth which has given birth to hundreds of ethnic groups and languages down the ages. It is also marked by a large number of cultures that are not found anywhere else in the world. Nevertheless, despite all the ethnic, linguistic and cultural variations found in it, this vast area has been looked upon by its neighbours from time immemorial as a region in its own right, as it abounds in broad commonalities that have kept its peoples united across time. For example, studies in historical linguistics have revealed the fact that the vast majority of South-East Asian languages either originated from common roots or have been long and inseparably interlinked. Besides, common views of gender, family structure, and social organization are clearly discernible throughout mainland and insular South-East Asia. In short, a distinctly common commercial and cultural inheritance has had its impact on the entire region for several centuries.

This region has also been heir to Hindu, Buddhist, Animistic, and Islamic traditions. Of the above major religio-cultural systems, Islam, being the youngest religion, was the last to enter and establish itself in it. In the course of time it emerged as a great cultural and political force. While doing so, it was not only greatly influenced, but also even considerably reformulated by the existing traditions of this region, namely Hindu, Buddhist and Confucian. But matters relating to Islam and Muslims in South-East Asia have been a neglected subject of study. The Muslims of this region have not got the same attention as their counterparts in West Asia got for various historical and geopolitical reasons. Moreover, the available Western sources of information about Islam and Muslims are far from being reliable as they are vitiated not only by their misconceptions about this religion, but also by their own neo-imperialist interests. An attempt has been made below to give a brief introduction about Islam and Muslims in South-East Asia.

Islam is the religion of millions of people in South-East Asia. The Muslim population is concentrated in what is known as the "Muslim Archipelago" extending from southern Thailand through Malaysia and Indonesia to the southern Philippines. The main characteristic of Islam in this region is that the cultural realities of South-East Asia derived from indigenous philosophies and different local traditions are adequately reflected in it. The Muslim countries of this region are briefly introduced below.

Malaysia

It consists of two different regions: Peninsular Malaysia on the Malay Peninsula at the southern extremity of the mainland of Asia and East Malaysia on the island of Borneo. It has a total area of 127584 square miles. To the north it is bordered by Thailand. In the south at the top of the Peninsula is the island republic of

Singapore. In the southeast across the Strait of Malacca is the Indonesian island of Sumatra.

Since the Malay Peninsula is situated at one of the great maritime cross-roads of the world, it has long been the meeting place of peoples from other parts of Asia. Malaysia is a multi-racial society. The Malays constituting about two-thirds of its population are overwhelmingly Muslims, who dominate the country in the political field. Their language called Bhasa Malaysia is the official language of the country. Among the other races, the Chinese make up about one-third of its peninsular population, while the peoples from South Asia, namely Indians, Pakistanis and Tamils from Sri Lanka constitute about 10% of its population. Thus this country presents a unique blend of three of the ancient and great civilizations-the Chinese-Buddhist-Confucian, the Indian Hindu and Malay-Muslim.

The spread of Islam in the Malay Archipelago was hastened by several important factors. It is said that merchants and sufis from India and Arab countries introduced Islam in this region which attracted both higher and lower classes of its population. This led to the emergence of several Islamic Malay kingdoms such as Perlak (now part of Indonesia) and Malacca which strengthened the roots of Islam. Malacca, a prosperous trading centre by virtue of its trade with China and the Muslim world, now became a great theological centre, from where Muslim preachers went to other Malay lands and spread the message of Islam. Mansûr Shãh (1458-77), the great ruler of Malacca, conquered all the Malay Peninsula upto the border of Burma and the central part of Sumatra. He liberally patronized '*ulama* and sufis. It was during his rule that the process of Islamization of Malaya was completed, following which Arabic script was adopted by its language, while Islam became the law of the land. The arrival of Islam was accompanied by the establishment of religious schools which provided education and literacy to the people. Side by side with teachers and '*ulama*, various Sufi orders also attracted the masses into their folds. For instance, the Naqshbandîyah Order still holds particular sway in the northern Malay states.

But later the fall of Malacca to the Portuguese initiated the new era of Western imperialism, following which the Malay world was divided and ruled by the British, Dutch, and Spanish, while Islam receded into the background. Thenceforth, the imperialists, particularly the British, encouraged the rapid growth of non-Malay immigrants mostly Chinese and Indians as labourers for tin mines and rubber plantations. This in turn forced the Malays to pay serious attention to maintenance of their own supremacy. And they took to Islamic revivalism as an effective tool for asserting their identity and leadership in their multi-religious society.

Indonesia

Indonesia is another important Muslim-majority country of this region. It is composed of some 13670 islands and covers an area of about 752,400 square miles. Petroleum, natural gas, tin, manganese, copper, nickel, bauxite, iron, sulphur, etc., are its main natural resources. As is evident from the available archaeological evidence and historical accounts, Islam was first brought to the ports of northern Sumatra by Indian Muslim merchants, traders and sufis in the thirteenth century, from where it spread to the remaining islands in the next two centuries by replacing Hinduism and Buddhism in a peaceful way, thereby adapting itself to the prevalent local values and traditions. The mystical Islam introduced in this land also stressed salvation of the individual through meditation and introspective personal piety rather than purification of the faith from extraneous elements. That is one main reason why strong Muslim communities are still found adhering to non-Muslim traditions and practices. The arrival of Islam there through the channel of traders and sufis was followed by the development of a markedly mystical religious literature, in which Muslim legends of saints were combined with Hindu-derived mythologies that constitute the traditional roots of Indonesian literature.

But during the 16th century the newly founded Muslim trading kingdoms could not forge unity and fought among themselves for supremacy. This not only weakened their position, but also enabled the Western colonial powers, namely the Portuguese, Spaniards, Dutch, and British, to occupy this area by sowing the seeds of dissension among the local rulers. And by the end of the 17th century the Dutch had established their full economic and political control over almost all Indonesian islands. This led to a marked decline of the indigenous Indonesian literature in the 18th and 19th centuries.

The very name Indonesia implies a nation of multi-religious adherents despite the fact that the Muslims comprising about 90% of its population are in the majority. It got independence from the Dutch colonial domination in 1949. It was also a major participant in the creation of the Association of South-East Asian Nations (ASEAN) in 1967.

Brunei

The state of Brunei meaning Abode of Peace is a small independent Islamic sultanate on the northern coast of the island of Borneo. Having an area of 2226 square miles, it is bounded to the north by the South China Sea and on all other sides by the East Malaysian state of Sarwak. It became independent in 1984 after having been a British protectorate since 1888. The Malays constitute about two-thirds of its population, while the Chinese number about one-fifths.

The official language of this country is Malay, while English is used here as a major second language. As elsewhere, the Malays are predominantly Muslims, while the Chinese are Buddhists, Taoists or Confucians. Islam reached this country in the 15th century. Awang Alak Betar became its first Muslim ruler. He embraced Islam in 1425, and adopted the Muslim name of Muhammad while on a visit to Malacca to meet Sultãn Muhammad Shãh, who introduced him to the fundamentals of this religion. During his rule the distinguished Arab scholar and preacher Sultan Barakat visited Brunei and devoted himself to the preaching of Islam, due to which it spread throughout the length and breadth of this country. The sultan of Brunei was so much impressed by Barakat that he married his daughter to him.

As is well-known, the economy of Brunei is totally dependent on its vast resources of petroleum and natural gas. Being one of the world's wealthiest oil-producers, it has developed a very rich and affluent society. Rubber, natural gas and timber are the other major exports of this country.

Muslims as a Sizable Minority in the Philippines

In addition to the above, Muslims constitute sizable minorities in several other countries of this region, namely Philippines, Thailand, Singapore, southeast Cambodia and southern Vietnam. Of them the Philippines has been an abode of Islam since the 14th century. Earlier, almost the whole of the southern Philippines had been under the Muslims. But in the course of time the Portuguese, Spanish and American colonialists conquered and subjugated them, thereby giving birth to what is known as the Moro problem which has defied solution ever since.

The Filipino Muslims constituting about 10% of the population of that country were called by the Spaniards as Moros because their religious practices resembled those of the Moors of Muslim Spain. They are generally poor and backward. They are concentrated in the southern provinces of Mindanao and Sulu, while the Christian Filipinos are settled in the islands of Luzon and the Visayas. When the Spaniards began their colonization of this country n 1565, they seemed to take revenge on the Muslims by suppressing them to a considerable extent for the earlier occupation of Spain by Arab Muslims for several centuries. It was the main reason that they have since remained poor and backward. Had it been another European country, the tone and style of their administration might have been different.

The main cause of the current Moro problem was that when the Philippines was granted independence by the United States in 1945, the Moros were treated as second-rate citizens and their administration was transferred to the Christian Filipino elite. This not only adversely affected their interests and welfare, but also put them in a state of subjugation. Thus the antagonistic situation caused for the Moros by various colonial policies not only prohibited them from pursuing and realizing their politico-religious aspirations, but also created in them a general feeling of alienation and unrest. This in turn compelled them to embark upon the course of confrontation. As such they formed in 1960s the Moro National Liberation Front which has been fighting incessantly for autonomy and independence. And that is still a burning problem.

Spurt in Evangelical Activities and Islamic Resurgence

It is worthy of mention in this context that Islam in this region was by and large unaffected by the religious reform movements that took place from time to time in the Middle East. This region witnessed Islamic resurgence for the first time following the spurt in evangelical activities launched by Christian missionaries in the wake of the arrival of the Western colonial powers in the 15th and 16th centuries, who not only preached Christianity, but also systematically confused and distorted Islam.

Since the memories of the years of the Crusade wars, occupation of Spain by Muslims for several centuries and the siege of Vienna in the 15th century by Muslim Turks had been quite fresh in their minds, they took to proselytization work with all the means at their command. Their activity was not confined to the non-Muslims alone, but they tried to convert Muslims also by advocating a policy of 'emancipation of Muslims from their own religion'. But the Muslims remained firm in their commitment to Islam. This led to a race between Islam and Christianity in South-East Asia. The Muslims viewed this development as a threat not only to their religious and cultural identity, but also to their political dominance. And they took to Islamic revivalism as a means of fighting this menace, for they saw no better way of safeguarding their interests than through Islamic resurgence. Thus the movement of Islamic revivalism in South-East Asia was mainly a political reaction to evangelical activities of the colonial West.

Even after their independence the Muslims, mostly the common people under the influence of the *ulama* stuck to the policy of Islamic revivalism. This simultaneously forced non-Muslim groups also to turn to their own religions with a view to maintaining their identity and strengthening their cultural traditions.

It is obvious from the above that the movement of religious resurgence triggered by the arrival of colonial powers in this region not only created and widened the gulf between different religious communities, but also severely struck at the roots of the age-old common bonds that existed among them from ancient times. For example, peace and security of this region is endangered by the Moro problem in the Philippines and by the devoutly Muslim, resource-rich province Aceh's bloody separatist dispute. Needless to say that independence for Aceh would not only signal the breakup of Indonesia, but also threaten regional stability.

Conclusion

In conclusion it may fairly be said that Islam has been a great cultural and political force in South-East Asia, and that the Muslim countries along with the Philippines, Singapore and

Thailand are progressing and moving up in comparison to the remaining states of this region, namely Cambodia, Laos, Myanmar, and Vietnam which are among the world's poorest countries. But notwithstanding these facts, no serious attention has so far been paid by scholars to study the literary, cultural and artistic heritage of these peoples. Thus there is need to undertake in-depth studies and research on Islam and Muslims in the multi-religious and pluralistic South-East Asian region in the true historical perspective.

In addition to the above, ethnic polarization caused by religious antagonism in recent times at the cost of philosophical and spiritual aspects of different religions in various parts of this region as well as the modern cultural and civilizational trends stimulated by both indigenous and neo-colonialist forces also deserve our attention in order to be able to delineate the factors that have led to intensification of tension in this contemporary culturally rich but economically and technologically backward region. Finally, the need to further study the broad commonalities that have kept its peoples united through the ages cannot be overemphasized. Thank you for giving me a patient hearing.

NOTES AND REFERENCES

1. M.B. Hooker (edited), *Islam in Southeast Asia*, Leiden, 1983.
2. *Encyclopaedia Britannica*, Vol. 27.
3. Deliar Noer: "Evangelical Activities in Southeast Asia" in *The Muslim World Leagure Journal*, Saudi Arabia, Vol. 21, No. 7 (January 1994), pp. 55-58.
4. Rhudora Bucoy: "The Moro National Liberation Front - An Empirical Study" in *The MWL Journal*, Vol. 16, Nos. 9&10 (January 1989), pp. 51-54.
5. Asghar Ali Engineer (edited), *Islam in South and Southeast Asia*, Delhi, 1985.
6. Inamullah Khan, *World Muslim Gazetteer*, Karachi, 1964.